# TURKISH MINIATURE PAINTING

# The Ottoman Period

First Published in 1974
Revised new edition (1978)
Dost Yayınları
Ahmet Rasim So. 15/5, Çankaya - Ankara, Turkey

Art Editor : Salim Şengil

Printed in Turkey by
Duran Ofset Matbaacılık ve Ambalaj Sanayi A.Ş. İstanbul

# Metin And

# TURKISH MINIATURE PAINTING

### Sixty-four Miniatures in full colour
### and fifty-three black and white illustrations

**DOST YAYINLARI**
**ANKARA**

## Abreviations for Collections

BM    The British Museum (London)
BN    Bibliothèque Nationale (Paris)
CBC   The Chester Beatty Library Collection (Dublin)
İÜK   İstanbul Üniversitesi Kütüphanesi (The Library of The University of İstanbul)
TİEM  Türk - İslam Eserleri Müzesi (İstanbul) - Museum of Turco - Islamic Works
TSM  Topkapı Saray Müzesi (İstanbul) - Topkapı Palace Museum  H = Treasury Library;  R = Revan Library; R = Revan Library;  B = Bagdad Library;  A = Ahmed III Library;  D = Documents from Topkapı Palace Archive;  E. H. = Emanet Hazinesi.)

## INTRODUCTION

The study and appreciation of Turkish miniature painting is a new thing. The reason why Turkish miniature painting has been thus neglected lies probably in the fact that until very recently it has been a closed book to the outsider. Many of the paintings have perished. The ones which have survived were in the possession of Sultans, therefore in finely bound manuscript volumes safely guarded in palaces to which there were difficulties in gaining access. Until quite recently there have been no publications revealing their contents. Similarly the lack of sources concerning aesthetic theories about the miniatures and the scarcity of documents revealing the biographies of artists and their methods of creation have imposed further restrictions on the scope of scholastic inquiries and stylistic analysis.

The pioneers in this field, who were not able to grasp the distinct and unique artistic qualities of Turkish miniatures, are not to blame, as they had access only to a very limited number of examples. Because of this they tended to concentrate on the painting of other Islamic cultures, mainly Persian. During the past two decades, there has been a marked change in point of view, especially on the question of Persian influence, and students of Islamic art have become aware of the equal importance of the Turkish painting.

A look at the contributory causes of the awakening of interest in the study of Turkish miniature painting calls for mention of the increasing cultural exchange among nations and the superior tourist facilities which assist the dissemination of first-hand experience of certain objects of art. In addition are the growing appetite among the general public for experience of alien cultures and the perfection of the facility of coloured photography. All these have resulted in tremendous changes in attitude towards the subject. Colour slides have made possible the transference to classrooms, private houses or lecture rooms of the miniatures from their albums, where the small pictures were initially meant to be viewed by one or two people at a time. They can now be viewed in all their immediacy and subtlety by the student at his leisure. Miniatures have always had a personal and lyrical quality which can now be widely enjoyed and which may succeed in arousing the interest of larger numbers of amateur appreciators, and further promoting in them a wish to see the unique originals in their natural setting. There is an increase in the quantity, as well as the quality, of books reproducing miniatures available to the world public. In these days two of the most recent have been published by UNESCO. There is also an illustrated catalogue listing Turkish miniatures in the Chester Beatty Collection in Dublin, and another listing those to be found in the British Museum. Official support for artistic activity on a national basis as a source of prestige has led to the organization of exhibitions of national art treasures abroad. Such an exhibition was that which, under the name of "Art Treasures of Turkey" toured the U.S.A. in 1966. In addition the International Congress of Turkish Arts, as distinct from the Congress of Oriental Arts, or the Congress of Islamic Arts, was established. The first meeting was held in Ankara in 1959, followed by a second in Venice in 1963, a third in Cambridge, England in 1967, a fourth in Aix-en-Provence in 1971, and a fifth in Budapest in 1975. So Turkish arts in general and miniature painting in particular have found a following of enthusiastic students and scholars.

Some scholars have constructed a thesis on the false premise that, like any other Islamic country, Turkey condemned figural representation, and hence painting in the western sense could not exist in Turkey. However, the Koran does not contain a single word against figural painting. Objection arose as a result of Islamic purists collecting *hadis,* or the sayings of Muhammed, which were supposed to support the condemnation of figural representation. These have been used with considerable effect by religious legists *(fukahâ)* to forbid any kind of figural painting. This is connected not only with a fear of idolatry but with the more universal fear of rivalling Creation itself, which is the prerogative of God. [1] The word in Arabic for painter is *musavvir* which literally means 'fashioner' or 'form giver' It is also an appellation used in the Koran to denote God himself, the Creator. While figural painting always remained non-acceptable to the official religious establishment, the strict attitude weakened owing to many factors. Turks, like Persians, had a long tradition of representational arts from pre-Islamic times, and among them the instinct and gift for pictorial arts were so deeply implanted that figural painting was indulged in spite of clerical disapproval, and in the course of time representational art took root, most noticeably under the Ottomans. Another important factor is that, like other Islamic potentates, the Ottoman Sultans indulged painting to its fullest measure, inviting native and foreign painters to form

1 On the figural representation almost all the general works on Islamic art have commented on the problem. For a recent study with a most informative discussion followed by a considerable bibliography see Oleg Grabar, *The Formation of Islamic Art,* Yale University Press 1973, pp. 75-103; 221-222; also see Osman Keskioğlu, "Islâmda Tasvir ve Minyatürleri", *İlâhiyat Fakültesi Dergisi,* IX (1961), pp. 11-23; Rıfkı Melûl Meriç, *Türk Tezyini Sanatları,* İstanbul 1973.

a section of their court. The Sultans sought to leave to posterity some memorial of themselves and to commemorate their campaigns and victories, and their glorious achievements. As we shall see later there is a wealth of miniatures. The originals of almost all the illustrations in this present book, each one depicting human figures, are housed in Topkapı Museum, which alone contains some ten thousand miniatures. Not only miniatures of human figures but, in spite of the excessive prudery of Ottoman society, erotic and nudist themes were introduced to Turkish miniature painting. Of course rulers could own or commission such works without challenge from anyone and regardless of courtly prejudice, since the Ottoman Sultan was at the same time Caliph, that is, the leader of all the Islamic world. Outside the court, patrons could conceal illustrated manuscripts in the privacy of their houses. Two factors tending to encourage unclothed bodies and erotic themes can be adduced. Firstly Ottoman society especially was deemed to be more liberal, more permissive, with a new awareness of a life or luxury and dalliance, and the appealing treatment of the female form became the common artistic possession of many 18th century artists. The second factor arose from the subject-matter of the works to be illustrated. Love stories, love poems, bath scenes, angels bathing, justify the nudes as a subject. Apart from the fully-clad Adam and Eve on page 54, there is on page 85 a miniature depicting Adam and Eve naked with only the conventional fig-leaf guarding their modesty. In early times, to be more precise in the 16th century, the number of figures of nude women are meagre, one example is from the manuscript *Jamasb-Name* dated 1527 *[BM Add. 24962]* depicting three young naked girls partly draped, who are supposed to be the daughters of the jinns. Probably there existed more miniatures of this category which were unfortunaterly destroyed by fanatical puritans or even by the owners themselves. But in the 17th and 18th centuries there was a marked interest and stimulation in rendering young girls and men. Pairs of lovers and suggestive representations of erotic themes became a practice. Here we have included a few black and white examples of these. For example Fig. 1 *[TSM H. 2168]* depicting a nude woman leaning with her back against a slender tree, — the veillike transparent fabric seems delicately

to caress her thighs, enabling her private parts to be seen under an illusory concealment; similarly a branch across the blossoms of her breast scarcely covers it, — a certain element of narcissism is introduced. In Fig. 2 *[TSM H. 401]* depicting five nude *peris* bathing, three are in the water half exposed, the other two are standing, one fully exposed, the other covering her modesty with her hands. Fig. 3 *[IÜK T. 5502]* depicts a public bath scene with several nude women, one of them totally exposed. Two albums of bazar work *[BM Sloane 5258 (263) and BN Od. 6-8]* have two miniatures which are similar, depicting in flesh-tints a single woman bathing completely nude, with the only difference that in *[BM Sloane 5258 (263)]* she is partly covered with lather.

The 17th and 18th centuries are full of artists who are devotees of the cult of the female breast, among them Levni and Abdullah Buhari, two great artists of the 18th century. Their females are represented with half-exposed breasts of which the only purpose is obviously to increase the appeal of the nude by contrast. On page 96 *[TSM. H. 2164]* Levni's famous dancing girl is an example of, this. In the same album Levni's sleeping woman miniature displays the female figure in a seductive pose. A companion miniature to this by Levni on page 95 is a young man in the same pose, intoxicated and holding a flask of wine. This miniature shows the tendency of this period, in contrast with the masculine style of previous centuries, for artists to render the male form in a feminine way. The male, obviously yielding to homosexual tendencies, appears female. Though the lack of virility is a pervasive trait, yet in male nude figures this is not emphasized. For instance Fig. 4 *[TSM. B. 408]* depicts male nude figures bathing in a thermal bath, another bath scene with male nude figures can be found in a 16th century manuscript *Hünername* second volume *[TSM H. 1524]*. Again in the 17th and 18th centuries attractive, suggestive respresentations of love scenes, courtship games, the yearnings of young men and women showing a certain degree of intimacy became a practice, owing to the interest in the rendering of younger girls and men. Here are three examples: Fig. 5 *[TSM. H. 2168]* a young man

holding the girl by her waist; Fig. 6 *[TSM. H. 2165]* a lover caressing the face of his beloved, and the third one Fig. 7 *[BN. Od., 6-8]* more interesting, the young lover with a lute serenading his beloved who is looking from the window.

On the other hand there are some specimens which reach the borderline of indecency, tinged with eroticism or a form of repressed lasciviousness. For instance a 16th century miniature in manuscript *Marvels of Art and Nature [BM Harleian 5500]* appears to be a talismanic figure of a young prince having sexual intercourse with a naked woman. A good example of this is Atai's *Hamse*, manuscript with 43 miniatures *[TSM. R. 816]*. There is another copy with 9 miniatures *[TİEM no. 1969]*. The first one contains three erotic scenes which directly approach pornography. The same manuscript contains several other miniatures in a further category which can be called secret eroticism, where the erotic element is present but suppressed, it is the subject matter not its means of expression or depiction. These subjects conflict either with social customs or private taboos, such as adultery, illicit or perverse love and others. Here are some examples of miniatures in this vein in this manuscript: a woman's claim against her husband denying her feminine rights; a rake lifting the veil covering the face of a woman whom he thinks beautiful but he discovers with horror that she is an old woman and he

6        7

vows not to be a womanizer any more; and adultery scene where a woman discovers her husband with a maid-servant red-handed; a young man while courting with a young woman while at the same time fighting with a lion; a young woman with an old man frightened by a rat; a rake caught red-handed; an old woman seducing a young girl. There are other similar miniatures in other manuscripts. For instance in a manuscript *[İÜT T. 6624]* one depicts a scene where an insolent young man lifts the veil of a young woman in the presence of other women and children, and she pushes him away. In another manuscript *[İÜK T. 5502] and [BM. Or. 7094]* we find a miniature depicting the neighbourhood people and police raiding a bawdy house. All these must have been expected to have provoked strong protests from pious Moslems. However, just to be on the safe side and so as not to create displeasure among the fanatical section of the population, the Sultans and high-ranking persons of taste chose to keep their paintings concealed.[2] For instance, after the death of Vizir Kara Mustafa Paşa in 1644, five portraits of himself and his contemporaries were found in a secret room in his palace. These were immediately destroyed. [3] Though such unfortunate incidents were isolated, there were others involving the destruciton or partial mutilation of miniatures. Sultan Mahmud II, one of the strongest advocates of reform and westernization, attempted in his time to cause his portrait to be displayed in barracks, schools and official buildings. This provoked strong reaction in fanatic quarters. After he died, all these portraits were immediately removed from public view. [4] Unfortunately the destruction has been so immense that the actual material surviving, though still reaching to thousands, is sadly meagre in comparison to what once existed.

Today, among miniature collections, occasionally we find specimens which have been mutilated either by erasing or scoring through the faces of human figures, particularly women.

2. Mouradgea d'Ohsson, *Tableau général de l'Empire ottoman,* Paris 1788-1824, IX, pp. 339; 446-7.

3 Joseph von Hammer-Purgstall, *Geschichte der osmanischen Reiches,* Budapest 1827-35, III. pp.235-6.

4. Hafız Ahmet Lûtfi, *Tarih-i Lûtfi,* İstanbul 1290-1328,V,pp.50-52.

This is the case with *[TSM. H. 1562 and TİEM no. 1968]*. In the latter the faces have been obliterated with red paint. All this emphasises the negative attitude towards art.

There is, however, evidence of enlightenment in this quarter. Evliya Çelebi, the great traveller of the seventeenth century, tells us of an incident where the attitude is quite the opposite of negative. A wealthy but narrow-minded man bought a fine illustrated copy of Firdowsi's *Shahname* *(Şehname)*. However, because of his dislike of figural art, he chose to mutilate the book. When this news got about, he was sent for trial where the judge Melek Ahmet Paşa asked him in anger how he could find it in himself to destroy on the spur of the moment, a book in which each single miniature had taken the artist more than a month to create. Finding him guilty, he ordered the culprit to be fined the equivalent of the price of the book, which he had recently purchased in an auction in Bitlis. In addition, the judge ordered him to be beaten a thousand times, expelled from the army and submitted to the rough justice of the mob.

A wide range of figural representation, some employing unusual and unexploited media, such as expendable, perishable art objects were made in the shape of animals or human beings, for use in connection with public festivals. This process of creation, detached from fixed forms and the delusion of permanence, is de-aestheticized, or rather in it non-objects are objectified and listed in records, usually written in poetical style, or shown in miniatures. These representations are important from three points of view:

1. They furnish new evidence and provide additional grounds for belief in the existence of figural representation in Islamic countries, rectifying the misconception that such did not exist.

2. As most of these representations have sculptural

qualities, being all-round objects or some In three-dimensional works in motion, it shows that the Ottoman Turks had a sense of sculptural and pure visual form.

3. It also shows that the acts, modes and media of Turkish traditional artistic creation were already fairly modern.

Traditional Turkish artists did not worry about the theoretical distinction and hierarchies existing between the fine arts, minor arts and utilitarian media. Today modern Western artists are attracted to certain activities which have long been regarded as minor arts or de-aestheticised media uniting art with technology and craftmanship.

So the illustration of manuscripts was only one form of Turkish representational art. Apart from book illustration, to rectify any misconception in this matter let us glance at some evidence of the existence of figural representation throughout the centuries :

☐ Seljuk architecture contains a large number of examples of sculptured figural stone reliefs frequently an organic part of the edifice, or even fused with it, such as human figures in singly or in pairs; certain fabulous creatures such as winged unicorns, winged sphinxes, eagles, antelopes, fishes and elephants were employed, often as symbols of royalty or saintly people. Here two examples are given. (Fig. 8) and (Fig. 9).

☐ Even sculpture in the round can be frequently seen on Seljuk-Ottoman tombstones. There are also rough sculptures of animal totems such as rams (Fig. 10), horses, birds and fishes, some of which today are exhibited in the museums of Van and Diyarbakır, and, the Ethnographical Museum in Ankara. [5]

☐ Calligraphy appeared as a major iconographical and ornamental device. Ottoman calligraphers were marvellously skilled in the weaving of patterns and the shaping of letters. The artist handles with complete assurance letter forms, through his medium creating from them human figures, ships, lions, camels, birds and mosques. Here four examples are given of figures made up calligraphically from words. A bird formed from *Bismillah* (Fig. 11); a lion made from the words meaning 'In the name of the lion of God, the face of God, the victorious Ali' (the lion symbolizing the strength of Ali) (Fig. 12); 'the perfect man', a composite figure in which a double 'Allah' forms the face, the shoulder part is formed by Hasan, Hüseyin, Muhammed and Ali, towards the legs is Fatma, and the chest

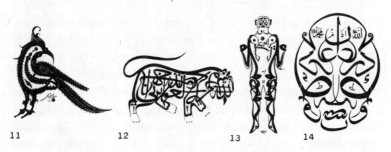

11          12                     13          14

5. On these see Nazmi Şevgen, "Anadolu'da at ve koyun motifli mezar taşları,," *TMO*, April 1955, no.1,pp.15-21; Hamit Zübeyr Koşay, "Doğu Anadolu Mezarlıklarında koç, at, balık ve koyun heykelleri", *Milletlerarası Birinci Türk Sanatları, Kongresi,* Ankara, 1962,pp.256-57, photos. CLXVII-CLXXIV. Also see Beyhan Karamağaralı, "The Order and Convent Art from XIIIth to XVIth Centuries in Anatolia," *İlâhiyat Fakültesi Dergisi,* XXI (1976) Ankara, pp. 277-284.

*Hu* is an attribute of Allah (Fig. 13); and a fourth figure is a face made up calligraphically (Fig. 14).

☐ Tapestry employed figures in some stylized forms to signify trees, various animals and even female figures. These schematic shapes, some of them no doubt remnants of tribal ideograms, are sufficiently differentiated as to allow definite identification. [6]

15                    16

☐ In the field of ceramic, glazed tiles, at which the Turks excel, there are abundant examples of figural representations. Although in the decoration of the ceramic object's surface, vegetal and geometric designs predominate, epigraphical, animal and human ones are used as well. A particular example of this involves Seljuk tiles made by the hundred in the thirteenth century. Kubad-abad summer palace is variously decorated with human figures sitting cross-legged (Fig. 15); with mythological animals such as birds in pairs (Fig. 16), harpies, sphinxes, dragons and hares; and more realistic animal forms like those of mountain goats, birds, lions, tigers, dogs, horses, donkeys and elephants. Ottoman ceramics also employ occasional figural designs such as the human form, stylized fish, birds and animals (Fig. 17 and Fig. 18), ships and other figures. In addition to these productions, Turkish ceramic workshops

6 See Şerare Yetkin, *Türk Halı Sanatı,* İstanbul 1974.

occasionally accepted special orders from foreign clientele to decorate ceramics with Christian subjects. A look at Seljuk coinage, brocades, ornated mirrors, or a lead eagle from a fountain, water issuing from a hole in its mouth, and its wings spread as in the Fig. 19 and other media provides further evidence of the use of figural representation. There are also painted glass objects with figural representations painted on them

17        18

such as some Seljuk glass flask fragments in the British Museum, middle of the 12th century. Also some late Ottoman dove-shaped perfume-flasks of opal glass. [7]

☐ Evliya Çelebi makes a distinction between two kinds of painter. The first type is the *nakkaş*, a word which is applied to miniature painters, illuminators, embroiderers, and also to those who painted wall decorations and floral designs. The second sort is the *musavvir* who were portrait painters. This classification of Evliya exhibits a certain ambiguity, as throughout the centuries the word *nakkaş* has been used for all types of miniature painter, including painters of portraits. But what is interesting here is that Evliya mentions that portrait painters were scarce in seventeenth century İstanbul, their number amounting to some forty and their activities spread over some four workshops. On the other hand, it seems from what Evliya

[7] For more details and colour illustrations see Fuat Bayramoğlu, *Turkish Glass Art and Beykoz - Ware,* İstanbul 1976.

tells us that mural painters were more popular. It was their practice to decorate the walls of their workshops with samples of their work to assist prospective customers to form an opinion of the quality of the artist's work. Although early examples of figural wall-painting have not survived to this day, we know that in Edirne, the third Ottoman capital, the palace had paintings executed directly onto the surface of the walls; while the publication of recent research and monographs tells us that throughout Turkey there are numerous examples of mosques, private mansions and even village houses, dating from the eighteenth through the nineteenth centuries, in which there are wall-paintings depicting in the main landscapes and architectural subjects with occasionally animal subjects and human beings.[8] Fig. 20 illustrates one of the wall paintings to be found in the Harem section of the Topkapı Palace.

19        20     21

☐ While on the subject of figural representation, one must also mention popular painting in early lithographed popular story books and large paintings intended for display on the walls of coffee houses.[9] An interesting genre is under-glass

8 On these see Rüchan Arık, *Batılılaşma Dönemi Anadolu Tasvir Sanatı*, Ankara 1976 (includes an English summary); Günsel Renda *Batılılaşma Döneminde Türk Resim Sanatı. 1700-1850*, Ankara 1977 (includes an English summary).

9 The two most important studies on these by Malik Aksel are: *Anadolu Halk Resimleri*, İstanbul 1960, and, *Türklerde Dini Resim*, İstanbul 1967 (includes an English summary).

painting, where figural representations and calligraphy are painted onto the back of the glass, with gold or coloured metal leaf applied to achieve a glittering effect. [10] The subject matter of under-glass painting is largely of a religious nature such as Fig. 21.

☐ There is one further category, however, of art in the making of books, which is filograms or the art of filigree in paper (or in leather for book covers) cut out as fine as lace or cobweb. These filograms were cut in series of sheets, each of a different colour, which were then laid one over the other on to a coloured background with exquisite lapidarian skill, reminiscent of the appliqué felt hangings and saddle cloths found in the tombs of the ruling chiefs of the Pazyryk nomads related to the Scythians of the High Altai, they are dating from the first century BC onward, and often representing mythical multi-coloured monsters with a human face, long-robed women, a rider approaching a figure seated on a throne, a lion-griffon and other such figures. [11] There are several albums representative of this art of filograms. For instance *[TSM H. 2153]* contains, besides abstract ornaments and calligraphy, also horses, plants, two different types of seven-headed dragons and trees. [12] Another album *[BN Or. 6-8]* contains fine specimens of filograms representing among other things a house and a devil. Another fine manuscript is *[İÜK T. 5461]* which contains several specimens of filograms of which we shall give more detail later.

☐ Another interesting field employing the representation of human figures is the shadow and puppet theatre. Only recently

10 See Malik Aksel, "Cam altı resimleri", *Türkiyemiz,* February 1972' no.6 (includes an English summary).

11 For illustrations see E.D.Phillips, *The Royal Hordes. Nomad Peoples of the Steppes,* London 1965, figs. 91,93,98 and 133.

12. For this album see Filiz Çağman, "XV. yüzyıl katı' oymacılık (kaat'ı eserleri", *Sanat Dünyamız,* September 1976,pp. 22-27 (includes an English summary).

have we discovered that there was not one but several kinds of shadow theatre and more than four distinct types of puppet. The best-known Turkish shadow theatre, Karagöz, used flat, two-dimensional figures, while the puppets of the marionnete theatre provided good examples of the use of three-dimensional sculpture. Among these types, mention should be made of giant puppets. These were large, puppet-like devices made of linen stretched over hoop frames, which represented various animals and human figures. They were operated from the inside and occasionally some of them were fitted with interior lighting equipment to facilitate their effective use at night. An illustration of two giant puppets, correct to scale, can be seen in the miniature on page 93. Other figures which appeared in this genre were sea monsters and other animals of fantasy like seven-headed dragons made of cast-iron and able to breathe fire.[13]

☐ Last but not least in this evidence of figural representation used by the Ottomans is a kind of expendable, perishable art object made in the shape of animals or human beings for display in connection with public occasions like festivals. Some examples of these were given by the present writer to the Third International Congress of Turkish Art in Cambridge in 1967 in paper entitled "A commonwealth of Turkish arts: the Ottoman Festival". Some of these manifestations can be referred to by the contemporary term 'kinetic art' i. e. an art that concentrates on movement and cybernetic sculpture. Two important fields of this kind where the Ottomans excelled were illumanations and fireworks. Splendid illuminations consisting of an elaborate network of thousands of lamps, some rigged on machinery which kept them in constant motion and all laid out so as to represent various figures and images, were displayed on special occasions. This pratice has survived even today, where during religious festivals lamps are sus-

13 See Metin And, *Karagöz. Théatre d'Ombres Turc,* Ankara 1977.

pended on ropes between minarets. Nowadays, the figural representations are not used, the lamps being arranged to spell out messages or quotations from the Koran.

☐ An almost equally important element was the pyrotechnic display. Fireworks were discharged from elaborate semi-theatrical structures representing castles, galleys, and dragons, also giants *(div-i anka)* and mermaids *(melaike-i derya)* dressed as human beings and other figural renderings. Mention should also be made of the processions of trade guilds in which certain figural objects, such as kites in the shape of birds, were flown or paraded. There was also a confectionery procession, during which several hundred figures and devices, all made of coloured sugar candy in the shape of human beings and all kinds of animals, were paraded. Some of these were small enough to be carried by one person while others were of a size which required them to be carried by four people or transported on wheeled carts. The figures represented in this way included the familiar animal forms of stallions, camels, giraffes, elephants, lions, leopards and tigers; bird figures like sparrow-hawks, pheasants and ducks; fantastic animal representations like sea-monsters and a bird-like figure having the head of a young man wearing a crown, and finally such inanimate objects as castles, fountains, candelabras, jugs, pitchers, vases and chess sets. [14]

Three documents in the Topkapı Palace *[D.10015, D. 10022, D. 9715],* giving the artists' names and accounts of expenses incurred for the festival of 1582 celebrating the circumcision ceremony of Sultan Murad III's son, provide very valuable information in this field. The artists parading shapes and ornaments sculpted in sugar were called *sükker nakkaşları,* and were in the main Jews. The documents go on to say that

14 On these see Metin And, *A History of Theatre and Popular Entertainment in Turkey,* Ankara 1963-64.

these artists received as a total payment for their work and for their tools 73, 977 *akçe* (an akçe is a silver coin, the chief unit of account in the Ottoman Empire). The total amount spent on the sugar sculpture was 366, 437 akçe while the figure expended on fireworks was 100,00 akçe.

An exhaustive list of evidence of the widespread use of figural representation in Turkish art would require a separate treatise on its own. This unfortunately is beyond the scope of our short survey in this text, which has necessarily had to confine its attention to book illustration of the old school of Ottoman miniature painting covering a period of five and a half centuries.

## HISTORICAL OUTLINE

The history of Ottoman painting may be outlined as follows. Broadly speaking, there have been four major cultural periods in the history of Turkish arts. Each of these periods has provided a distinctly different cultural setting for the development of these arts. The conditions under which the arts have developed within each period have been quite different. The first period is that of the pre-Islamic Central Asian and Ural-Altaic Turkic cultures from which the Turkish nation derives its origin. The people of those cultures were Manichean and Buddhist and practised animism and shamanism. Even before their conversion to Islam they possessed a fairly high level of civilization. From the ninth century onwards various Turkish rulers controlled at different times large sections of the Near and Middle East. Among them, the Turkish tribe Uygurs were esteemed for their more advanced civilization. They were practising the art of book painting as early as the eighth century. In 840, when the Kırghıs overthrew the empire of the Uygurs in the north, the latter emigrated to the territory of present-day Chinese Turkestan, which had already been settled by the Turks. Theirs was a culture which was influenced by Indian,

Chinese, Sassanid, Iranian and even Hellenistic styles, which being thoroughly assimilated, profoundly and for all time affected their painting. Another major cultural acquisition during this period came about due to the adoption of Islam throughout Central Asia in and after the seventh century. Transoxonia, Bokhara and Samarkand were important headquarters of artistic enterprise especially for painting. Strong evidence of the survival of this period's styles can be detected in the drawings and miniatures to be found in the so-called Albums of Mehmet the Conqueror housed in the Topkapı Palace Museum *[H. 2152-54 and H. 2160]*. Their origin and dating have long been the subject of scholarly discussion. [15] Although this is beyond the scope of our present survey, one may safely assume some of the drawings and miniatures in these albums to be definetely Turkish and of the fifteenth century. However the fact that not all are of the same period is obvious. Some features of Chinese painting have been grafted onto them, in addition to iconographical subjects traceable to Central Asian sources. The most interesting of them are by the hand of Siyah Kalem 'Black Pen', otherwise known as Muhammed Baksi Uygur, [16] whose rendering of the supernatural and surrealistic world through the medium of an earthly realism, especially in some details of human and animal anatomy, is unique.[16]

The second period in Turkish painting spans the civilization of the Seljuk Turks who, from the eleventh to the thirteenth century, settled on the Central Anatolian plateau. Though works of art in abundance have survived from the Seljuk period, yet among them are very few book illustrations. A thirteenth

15 See Richard Ettinghausen, "Chinese representations of Central Asian Turks", *Beiträge zur Kunstgeschichte Asiens. In Memoriam Ernst Diez,* İstanbul 1963, pp.208-222, fig. 11-13; E. Grube, "Herat, Tabriz İstanbul-The Development of a Pictorial Style", *Paintings from Islamic Lands* (Edited by R. Pinder-Wilson), Oxford 1969, pp.85-109.

16 On Siyah Kalem see Emel Esin, "The Turkish Baksi and the Painter Muhammad Siyah Kalam", *Acta Orientalia,* XXXI (1970),pp. 81-114.

century manuscript, *Varka and Gülşah,* is the most important document we have on Seljuk Turk miniature painting. [17] Persian and Byzantine painting have left a strong imprint on this work. In the post-Seljuk period, Anatolia was ruled by independent principalities in the different provinces. Very little is known about the painting done during this time. [18]

The third period, which forms the central topic of this survey, is the Ottoman period. While the fourth is the period of westernization, during which artists modelled their work on western painting. This dates from the beginning of the nineteeth century to the present time and developed at the expense of indigenous traditional miniature painting, which gradually ceased to exist. [19]

With the conquest of İstanbul on 29th May 1453 by Mehmet Mehmet II, the Conqueror, a new phase started, which also marked the beginning of third period in miniature painting. İstanbul, the fourth and last capital of the Ottomans, became the centre of culture and art dominated by the new capital's personality. The seventeenth century poet Nabi in his eulogy of İstanbul in the following couplet said:

Drawing and painting, calligraphy and gilding
Achieve beauty and grace in İstanbul.

Fatih Mehmet II, an enlightened Sultan, showed appreciation of the Renaissance burgeoning in Italy. Several Italian artists were invited to İstanbul: among them Matteo de Pasi, Costanzo da Ferrara, Gentile Bellini and Mastori Pavli. They

17 See Ahmet Ateş, 'Un vieux poème romanesque persan: récit de Warqah et Gülshah'', *Ars Orientalis,* IV(1961)pp.143-152.

18 On the pre-Ottoman Turkish miniature painting see. Oktay Arslanapa, *Turkish Art and Architecture,* London 1971 ,pp.308-313; K. Yetkin, *L'Ancienne peinture Turque du xııe au XVIIIe siecle,* Paris 1970,pp.7-18.

19 For Western influence see Adolphe Thalasso, *L'Art Ottoman* Paris (no date of publication); A. Boppe, *Les Peintres du Bosphore au Dixhuitième Siècle,* Paris 1911; Halil Edhem, *Elvah-ı Nakşiye Koleksiyonu,* İstanbul 1970.

were retained by the court and resided there, supported by the sovereign, whose twofold intention in this was, first, to have his portrait painted, thus breaking the Islamic prejudice against the use of figural images in art, and by doing this, he hoped to set an example to future generations of Turks. Secondly he hoped to educate native talents. Among the famous names of individual talents of his time are Sinan of Bursa, a pupil of Mastori Pavli, and Hüsamzade Sunullah of Bursa. [20]

After Fatih's time there were other European painters who visited Turkey. For instance during Süleyman I's reign, the Danish painter Melchior Lorck came to work in İstanbul. He has left more than a hundred paintings depicting İstanbul scenes and the person of the Sultan. These paintings are collected in several printed albums. In 1584, during Murad III's reign the historian, Johannes Lewenklau, came to İstanbul with the purpose of illustrating a book he had written on Ottoman history. In connection with this, he made more than a hundred paintings. However they were never published and now exist in a bound album of 185 folios in the National Bibliothek in Vienna [Cod. 8615]. Another painter, probably a Pole, stayed in İstanbul between the years 1588 and 1592 working at the residence of Ambassador Bartholamus Pezzen Heinrich Hendrowski. During this time, he painted the Sultan's court and Turkish life in 159 exquisetely executed coloured drawings. These were partly published recently [21] and the originals are kept today in an album of 172 folios in the National Bibliothek in Vienna [Cod. 8626]. These and the work of other European painters are most valuable as visual documents for students of Turkish painting from the point of view of first analysing how much Turkish artists have been influenced by the West

20 See Esin Atıl, "Ottoman miniature painting under Sultan Mehmed II", Ars Orientalis, IX (1973),pp.103-120,pls 1-12.

21 See Alberto Arbasino, I Turchi. Codex Vindobonensis 8626, Parma 1971.

and vice versa, secondly of soberly testing by means of this analysis the accuracy of topographical information supplied by these pictures and the likeness to the model in the portraits, in comparison with those done of the same subjects by Turkish artists.

From Fatih's time very little is still extant apart from a portrait of Fatih by Sinan; a surgical treatise *Jarrahiyyat al-khaniiyah* *[BN suppl. turc. 693]*, plus two copies of the same work both now in İstanbul. One in the İstanbul Millet Library *[no. 79]* and the other in the İstanbul Faculty of Medicine, Library of the Institute of History of Medicine *[T.Y.263]*. Two illustrations here are from the Millet Library copy (Fig. 22 and Fig. 23). An *İskendername* (Book of Alexander the Great) containing 20 miniatures *[BN suppl. turc. 309]* only three of which match in style the date of the manuscript; and *Dilsuz-name* (The Book of Compassion), containing 5 miniatures *[Bodleian Library (Oxford) no. Ouseley 133]* [22] which betray a very close resemblance to the Shiraz school.

Two manuscripts from the reign of Bayazid, the son of Fatih, have been handed down to us. One is *Khosrav and Shirin* by the poet Shaykhi *[Uppsala University Library no. Vet. 86]*. The style in the main is close to that of the school of Herat. The other is a pair of large miniatures of the *Süley-manname* (The Book of Solomon) by Firdevsi of Bursa *[CBC no. 406]*. Both of these works herald the emergence of a distinct Ottoman style. From this time onwards, it did not take long for works indigenous and genuinely Turkish in feeling to appear. Among the artists of this period two names are known: that of Ahmet Şibilizade of Bursa, a pupil of Sinan, and Baba Mustafa. Following the conquest of Tabriz by Selim I in 1514, sixteen artists were brought to Turkey from Persia and some

---

22 See Ivan Stchoukine, "Miniatures Turques du Mohammed II" *Ars Asiatique*, XV(1967),pp.47-50.

from Aleppo. Among them were Taceddin and his son, Hüseyin Bali. Also Hasan Çelebi who is best known as the deco-

22                                        23

rator of the walls of Topkapı Palace. These Persian artists were charged with the responsibility for passing their skill on to succeeding generations of artists. Yet despite their influence, the course of Turkish painting began to show unmistakeable home-grown traits.

During the reign of Süleyman I. known as 'the Magnificent', Turkish miniature painting reached its zenith. A document dated 1527-28 *[TSM. D. 932]* shows there were 29 master painters and 12 apprentices attached to the Court. Out of 29 artists 14 were Turks. The rest comprised several Persians, and some Albanians, Circassians and Moldavian artists. The chief master of this group was Şah Kulu of Tabriz. Mention should also be made of the names of Ali Nakkaş, İbrahim Çelebi, Kıncı Mahmut, Memi Çelebi, Abd el Feta and Hasan Kefeli. However the most meritorious and versatile artist of this time was Nasuh el silâhi el Matraki, better known as Matrakçı Nasuh. We are indebted to Professor Hüseyin Yurdaydın of the University of Ankara for his long research on Matrakçı Nasuh. Through his efforts we know that at least three lavishly illustrated manuscripts are the product of his hands. Matrakçı Nasuh was not only considered the foremost and unique historico-topographical painter, but was also famed as a warrior, a historian, a mathematician, a set designer for dramatic war games and [23] a champion of *matrak* which is a form of fencing with wooden swords practised as a dance, in which the swordsman uses a small round cushion as a shield. Another product of this reign was the *Süleymanname* (The Book of Süleyman I) containing 69 miniatures *[TSM H. 1517]* dated 1558, of which three miniatures are included in this book on pages 44, 45 and 46. Professor Nurhan Atasoy of the University of İstanbul has attributed at least some of the miniatures in the *Süleymanname* to a painter of Hungarian origin called Macar Nakkaş Pervane. [24]

From the time of Selim II, we know only one artist's name. He is Reis Haydar, known as Nigari, who is responsible for three fine portraits. But in the reign of Murad III, Turkish miniature painting reached another apogee. Among the artists of this time were Ali Çelebi, Molla Kasım, Mehmet of Bursa, Mehmet Bey, Molla Tiflisi, Hasan, Suni and the Persian Veli Can. The most distinguished and prolific artist was Üstat Osman. Among the vast number of works by him, mention should be made of *Hünername* (The Book of Accomplishments) which was in four volumes, two of which have survived. Most of the miniatures are by Osman helped by his workshop. Several colour reproductions in this present book are from *Hünername*. He seems to have been especially noted for his portraits of Sultans. Another important artist of this period is Lütfi Abdullah, the chief master, under whose supervision six volumes of *Siyer-i Nebi* (The Acts of the Prophet), five of which have survived, contained more than eight hundred miniatures. He also illustrated an earlier work, *Acaib el Mahlûkat* (The Marvels of Creation) in 1575. The most prolific period in the

23 On the scenery and dramatic mock battles among the Ottomans see Metin And,"Türklerde dekor sanatı ve dramatik savaş gösterileri", *Türkiyemiz,* June 1972 no. 7 (includes an English summary).

24 See Nurhan Atasoy,'1558 tarihli Süleymanname ve Macar Nakkaş Pervane", *Sanat Tarihi Yıllığı,* III, İstanbul 1970,pp.167-196.

history of Ottoman miniature painting is the 16th century, during which it attained greatest distinction. Manuscripts containing hundreds of miniatures in the Turkish style were produced throughout the century.

In the seventeenth century, though some fine manuscripts were produced, the art might be said to have been in decline if contrasted with that of the previous century. It simply does not have the grandeur and monumentality of sixteenth century art. During the reigns of Ahmet I and Osman II, the best known painters were Nakkaş Hasan, Ahmet Nakşi, Kalender Paşa and Mir Seyit Mehmet. Among the painters of the reigns of Murat IV and İbrahim I Evliya mentions the name of Pehlivan Ali, Osman, Ahmet Osman and İbrahim Mahmut. Evliya also gives other information regarding painters of his time, mentioning the names of Miskali Solakzade and Tiryaki Osman as the most distinguished painters of battle scenes. According to him, there were in İstanbul 1000 painters and 100 workshops at the time.

The next Sultan, Mehmet IV, seems to have been a self-professed patron of arts. Under his patronage a certain brief revival appears to have taken place. Among the artists of his reign were Derviş Ali, who worked in Edirne, and a painter by the name of Hüseyin, who painted a genealogical book *Silsilename* dated 1692, now in the possession of the Vakıflar Genel Müdürlüğü, Ankara. Hüseyin Gilani painted another manuscript of the *Silsilename* during the reign of Ahmet II. This is kept in Vienna *[Nationalbibliothek Cod. A. F. 17]*. In the same library there is a third genealogical book illustrated by Hasan el Musavvir (Rıdvan), entitled *Sübhat el ahbar* (The Rosary of Information) *[Nationalbibliothek Cod. A.F. 50]*. Another painter by the name of Mustafa Nakşi was responsible for the illustration of the manuscript known as *Hottinname* (The Book of the Conquest of Hotin).

Although the seventeenth century saw the production of

some books on divination, on genealogy, others of sacred nature and some chronicles, yet most of the artists of this period preferred to paint individual miniatures complete in themselves rather than illustrations for books. Sometimes the outer margin of these single sheets is of marble paper and sometimes it is sprinkled or elaborately figured with gold. They have then been frequently put together and bound in albums called *murakka* so that they can be more easily and more exclusively enjoyed than minatures which are part of a larger whole or manuscript. By this time, in contrast to the style of miniature painting, drawings, usually faintly tinted with gold and colours, were tending to become the vogue. The constant or recurring themes in these drawings were sketches of winged creatures called *perisor* genii, and loving couples caught in an idyllic mood. The figures of young men and young women, beautiful concubines and animals exist side by side with floral designs. Horses and dogs are portrayed very realistically as in a particular case which comes to mind of a worn-out, sorry horse whose ribs seem just about to burst through his fleshless hide *[TSM H. 2165]* (Fig. 24). On the other hand, birds are more or less stylized. All these combine with some Chinese, Persian and European features.

The output of the seventeeth century can be assumed to have provided the formative influence on eighteenth century artists, especially on Levni, as would be best illustrated by a 17th century drawing with color depicting a young man lying holding a wine bottle *[TSM H. 2135]*, heralding a century earlier the miniature of Levni reproduced on page 95. Levni was the most prominent artist of the time, dominating that period, 'the Tulip Era', so called because love and care for tulips became increasingly the vogue. The tulip symbolises the luxury, extravagance and gracefulness of this period. Abdülcelil Çelebi of Edirne, better known as Levni, was responsible for two volumes of *Surname* (The Book of Festival). However, he was more concerned with single paintings depicting individuals. Those single leaves bear elegant drawings of beautiful girls, languid ladies in reclining positions, charming young men and a portrait of the reigning Sultan, Ahmet III, who was the painter's patron. Levni's work was distinguished by a mastery of line, of elegant and flexible contours, and the richness of detail with which he endows garments, employing intricate designs, pleats and folds. On the other hand in his faces, which · are expressionless and stereotyped, certain mannerisms can be noted.

24                                                                                  25

The other prominent painter of the eighteenth century is Abdullah Buhari, who painted subjects similar to Levni, but showed marked stylistic changes tending more towards European painting: *[İÜK T. 9364 and TSM H. 2143]* and single sheets such as *[TSM YY 1043, 1086, 1042]*. Other names of painters in this century are Seyyit Yümni, Kayyum Baş and some Christian names such as Refail, Konstantin, Istrati. These last mentioned artists, paintings are collected in *[TSM H. 2143]* . Towards the end of the eighteenth century, European influence became rather more noticeable but it never came to predominate. However this period was the beginning of the end of miniature painting. For instance two manuscripts executed towards the end of the eighteenth century, *Hubanname* (The Book of Beauties) with 39 miniatures and *Zenanname* (The Book of Women), with 44 miniatures *[İÜK T. 5502]* betray a pronunced European character. Of the latter manucript there is another copy with 40 miniatures [BM. Or. 7094]. They feature portraits of women of different nationalities together with scenes taken from daily life such as women bathing, an accouchement in the harem, a raid on the neighbourhood bawdy house and an excursion undertaken by women. Similarly books of costumes were another favorite subject of this period. One album having 98 water colours depicts various people of different ranks in their appropriate costumes [TSM A. 3690] and a later copy of it has 32 water colour miniatures [IÜK T. 9362]. These late period artists seem to have a interest in landscapes, as in Sefaretname-i İran (The Book of the Persian Embassy) which has 31 miniatures of pure landscape depicting towns from İstanbul to Teheran [İstanbul Millet Library no. 822], in which human figures are not shown, here we have reproduced the miniature on İzmit (Fig. 25) and Amasya (Fig. 26). In contrast to these miniatures devoid of all human figures, landscape used a great deal in portraiture either as background, or as an ornament on the outer margin of the portraits. There are several manuscripts containing portraits of Sultans depicting the complete Ottoman dynasty from the first Sultan to the last [TİEM 1976 - İstanbul Süleymaniye Library no. Nafiz Paşa 1183 - TSM E. H. 1435 - BM Or. 9505 - Konya Mevlana Museum-Berlin Staatsbibliothek Or. fol 4113, Or. fol 3064 and Or. quart 1828]. Similarly Tasvir-i Süfera (Portraits of Ambassadors) featuring portraits of Turkish ambassadors [İÜK T. 4422 - İÜK T. 9363 and İstanbul Archaeological Museum no. 401] and the portrait of Selim III with his vizir Koca Yusuf Paşa shows the increasing presence of European stylistic influence. Western influence is particularly noticeable in the painter's technique in the portrait of Princess Fatma ,daughter of Abdülmecit executed in 1850 by a painter Ruben Manas (Fig. 27). (continued on page 97)

26

27

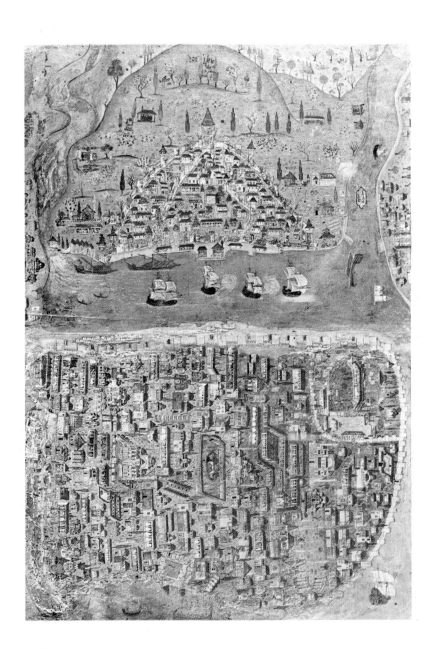

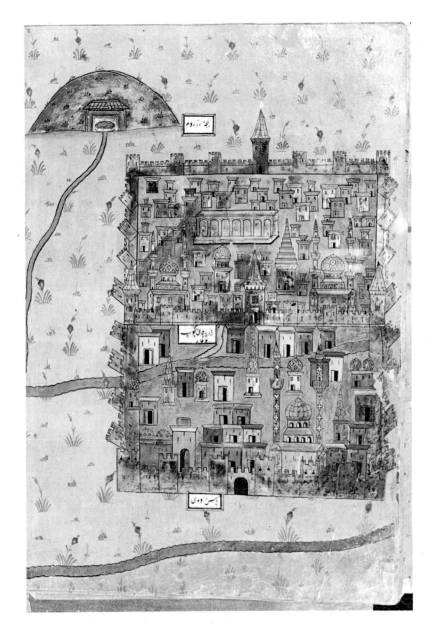

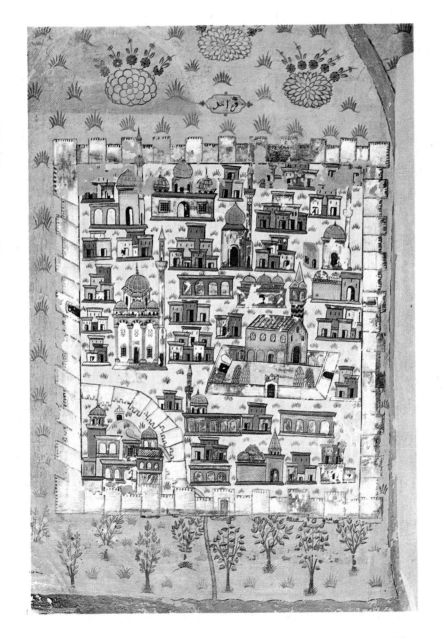

45

50

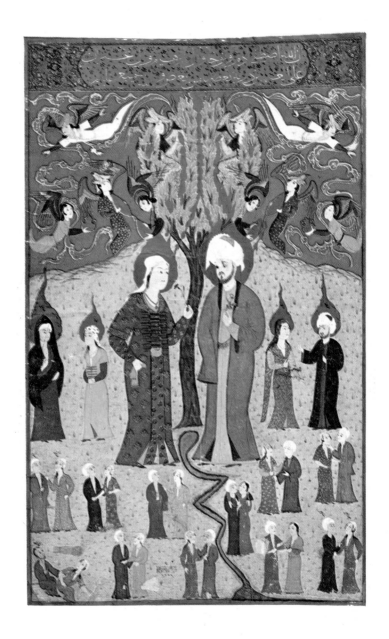

54

56

مولانا سلطان العلمانك زيارتنه وارمشيدى زيارتق مالامش
كلورکن اوکوذ همان سولٰان كوب عجم حذمتنه وارب بويننى يرو

جذالحركت انيوبه بالدى حضرت مولانا مبارك انى ارقه سنده دوردى
سورى بارغشه دى د الصفات ايلدى بعده قضايلرك كلوب بولادرلرا

83

(continued from page 32)

## STYLE, TECHNIQUE AND THE SOCIAL POSITION OF THE ARTISTS

Turkish miniatures have such an individuality of their own that they are easily distinguished from other Islamic paintings. Though they lack the subtlety, delicacy and refinement of the Persian painting, they have vigour and the quality of simplicity. The spirit of Persian painting is in many ways foreign to the Turkish. While the Persian artist shows an appeal to subjectivity, romanticism, lyricism and artificiality, the Turkish artist's approach reflects objective truth and in his work a certain realism steals in. The Turkish artist states all the facts clearly in the boldest and broadest banner. He achieves the maximum of expression through the minimum of means.

The most stylistic and iconographical characteristic is a preoccupation with preconceived ornamental composite forms with decorative conventions, especially in the courtly scenes. These are elaborate compositions, crowded with figures, blossoming trees, patches of flowers, variegated foliage, elaborately embroidered tents or brocade robes, intricate ornamentation of the background architecture, even of the ground. Many of the colour reproductions in this book, especially the ones selected from *Hünername*, may serve to illustrate this richness of ornamentation.

Though Ottoman miniatures shared much in common either directly or indirectly with previous styles like those of the Persian, the Central Asian Turkish and the Occidental styles, these influences were felt only in a general sort of way and did not obliterate local elements. The best specimens of Turkish miniatures possess a quality of frankness, vitality and vigour which is not seen in other Islamic paintings. However, the origin of some forms and conventions in Turkish painting can hardly be held in doubt. They were derived from Islamic painting. For example shadowing, foreshortening and the third dimension have not commanded the attention of the Turkish artist or of his colleagues in other Islamic countries. The viewpoint is usually more elevated than the actual scene so that the perspective of the scene or building is visualised as it would appear from above. Within this aerial perspective the visual relationship between objects (laws of scale and proportion) is consciously ignored by the artist. Hence large objects such as trees and mountains are reduced in scale in order to exhibit them complete in the scraps of space left vacant by the principal subjects of the picture. Nor is there any attempt to make diminished objects appear distant. So the artist fills his picture in, not by adhering to the proportions of the objects as they actually are but by a broad emphasis on the main actor in the drama held in integral relation to the other figures. When he is featured, the focus of attention is on the Sultan. For example, in the miniature on page 74, among the decapitated enemy heads we can differentiate one in the center wearing a crown which is much larger than the others in the foreground. Similarly the conspirator against the Sultan in the picture on page 75 is a giant-size figure. Likewise in the miniature on page 79 depicting Mevlana Jalal-al-din Rumi standing, where his face is more prominent in proportion to his body and to the faces surrounding him. Also in the miniature on page 55, Noah standing on the stern rudder of the Ark appears giant sized comparad to his seven sons on board the Ark, as well as in proportion to the Ark itself. And likewise in the miniature on page 54, Adam and Eve and their progeny consisting of thirteen twins of both sexes can exemplify this well, where Adam and Eve appear several times bigger than all their twin children.

As a result of all these, sometimes a miniature depicts a world where the law of gravity does not apply. Occasionally objects do not seem to be touching the ground. The Turkish artist employs stereotypes of gesture and grouping and a restricted number of formal postures in the rendering of figures.e.g. standing, sitting, fighting, falling etc. Usually, for instance, rows of people in the foreground turn their backs to the Sultan as well as to the centre of action so that they face the viewer of the miniature (See miniatures on pages 47, 58, 68, 69 and 70).

Any reader who examines carefully the minatures in the present book will discover another aesthetic feature—albeit a negative one, the total absence of facial expression. The suppression of interest in character and expression is a conscious effect on the part of the artist. In scenes of executions, battles and massacres swimming in bloodshed, also when a Sultan receives a mortal wound and is dying, the surrounding faces show a complete indifference; no scow, no smile or grief, not even a wrinkle, the subjects being types rather than individuals. Occasionally certain signs of expression such as humour are noticeable. For instance in the portrait of Nasreddin Hoca, the great Turkish humorist *[TSM H. 2142]* where he is wearing an enormous turban, riding on a small donkey, his amused facial expression fits to perfection his legendary character.

One will notice that something very rare in Turkish miniatures is the sense of motion. Most of the miniatures are static with the forms frozen in a hieratic convention. Yet some hunting scenes, battles, armies marching, the processions on horseback and on foot, boats sailing in the water, all set against an immobile environment, imply a suggestion of movement of round, or plane or straight formation. Some of the processions are depicted in a straight formation such as the ones on pages 49, 87 and 94, and some in round, or sinuous from such as the one on page 86. What the Italian artists called *contrapposto,* that is counter-balancing of any movement of the left or to the fore by a compensatory movement to the right or the rear, rarely exists in Turkish miniature painting. Yet a sense of mevement is emphasized by the suggestion of the swaying movement of the dancers, for instance in pages 57, 90, 91, 92, and 96, or on page 81 of the ship caught in a whirlpool, by the various fishes, mermaids, serpents and water creatures. Likewise, in the miniature on page 55 depicting Noah's Ark amid the Flood, with Noah's seven sons looking out in different postures, the turbulence of large waves creates a sense of movement. Another feature of this miniature, like the one on page 81 and 83, is that they are devoid of any framing. Figures cutting right through the frame of the composition are a salient feature in many miniatures. Lack of correct anatomy, representation of light and shade or, correct perspective, no suggestion of atmospheric tone or mood, a refusal to use a darker colour to represent the cast of shadow are also characteristic. Instead of sober and low-toned contour, all is glowing with lucent distinctness even in some miniatures depicting starry nights. This style which is marked by the total lack of roundness, depth of tone and aerial perspective, where the object being represented is shown as absolutely flat, is characteristic of all Islamic painting. Yet the flat style was modified after the middle of the 17th century by the Europeanized school of artists who frequently introduced slight line shading, a sense of relief and roundness emphasized especially by reticent high lights on salient features especially in pleated and draped contours. Whereas earlier artists used little modelling of draperies, a feeling for plasticity becomes noticeable, especially sinuous curves of bodies in movement or in repose. A felicitous vitality of line drawing is the characteristic of some of the individual miniatures in the albums of the late 17th and 18th centuries. This can best be illustrated by a drawing depicting above two rams, and below two wrestlers fighting [TSM H. 2135]. The earlier lack of mood and atmosphere has been modified where the favourite subjects of the later period demand a lyrical and idyllic mood. European influence is also particularly noticeable in the treatment of perspective in the late period, especially in some miniatures depicting landscape or indoor portraiture.

The beauty of the Turkish painting lies in its rhythmic contours (*tarh*) as well as its colour appeal. Vibrant colours, like crimson red, magenta, blues and greens of several hues which seem to penetrate the eye, are the colours used by the Turkish painters. Each object has its own and proper colour, applied plainly and without any change of hue. The pigments used are mostly vegetable extracts, treated with white of egg and other ingredients. Another characteristic is the liberal use of black, white and gold paints. Gold is used not only for illumination and ornament, windows, pillars of pavilions and the borders of the paintings, but as a background in lieu of sky and for inscriptions. Most delicate lines are employed to refine the edges of coloured areas, rendering clarity of shape and conciseness of expression. The composition of the groupings of the figures (*meclis*) and the certain symmetry in this (*endam*), have been fairly well thought out, often as a concept of design.

The painters employed in the execution of these miniatures constituted a workshop working under the direction of a single master (*sernakkaş* or *nakkaşbaşı*). Individual differences of style are apparent, but it is not easy to pin down the particular artist to a particular style as often the miniatures are not signed. Probably, the *nakkaşbaşı* planned each illustration, then allotted some subjects to his pupils and assistants. He would impose his will on the painters who worked under his direction. A good example of this is seen in two albums from Topkapı Palace Museum [*A. 3593 and A. 3594*]. In the present book we have included a few miniatures from the former of these albums (see miniatures on pages 86, 87, 88-89, 90, 91, 92, 93 and 94).

These depict a public festivity lasting fifteen days and fifteen nights which took place in 1720. In comparing the two albums, both executed by Levni's workshops, there is a certain similarity in the draughtsmanship and coloring, yet a slight difference in style. While the former album is definitely executed Levni's style, the latter does not seem to show complete uniformity and distinctness. Some of its illustrations are no more than hasty, crude drawings and they appear to have been colored by different hands.

It is a plain fact that several hands were engaged in the making of a manuscript book. These would include the author, the calligrapher (*hattat*), the gilder, the illuminator (*müzehhip*) who worked up the intricate frontspieces and designed chapter headings and other subsidiary ornaments, the margin drawer (*cedvelkeş*), the illuminator of intricate floral ornamentation (*girih-bend*), the gold-beater, the gold mixer, the illuminator in charge of sprinkling gold on the borders (the work itself was called *zerefşan*), marbled paper maker (*ebru* maker), the illuminator of floral designs by paper-cutting (*ezhar-şükûfe kat'ı*), the painter (*nakkaş* or *ressum*), the master binder (*mücellid*), and the artist who ornamented the bindings with lacquer work (*rugni*, the work itself was called *rugan*, later Edirnekâri).

Although the preparation of an illuminated manuscript is a collective work where the various craftsmen were engaged in keeping pace with their colleagues in producing a fine work, there are exceptions. For instance, Matrakçı Nasuh, mentioned earlier, was author and draughtsman and colourist of his works. Since he is known to have been a good calligrapher, probably his whole manuscripts were his sole work. Another example of this can be found in a manuscript already mentioned of the 17th century [*İÜK T. 5461*] of 120 pages by Mahmud of Gazne (who should not be confused with Mahmud, Sultan of Ghazni and conqueror of India on the tenth century) [25] where he has written the poems in the manuscript, the calligraphy, the treatment of the paper, the subsidiary ornaments such as the binding, the illustrations and miniatures are all his own work. His miniatures include vases of flowers surrounded by fruits such as pears, cherries, figs and grapes, also a few landscapes and kiosks with a sense of perspective, some fine filograms, even a collage of flowers where the hearts of flowers consist of various seals.

All these above were considered craftsmen (*ehl-i hiref*), since art was still simply regarded as one of the manual crafts in much the same way as that of goldsmiths or bricklayers. The craftsmen were united in guilds, with those professions with whom they had some sort of craft connection. Each had a patron saint. (Evliya informs us that the patron saint of *nakkaşan* was *Şemrahim*), and each obeyed the rigid rules which governed the guilds. The master (*kethuda*), the journeyman, (*serbölük*) and the apprentice (*şakird*) each fixed in a rigid hierarchy, formed the workshop organization. The training of the painter followed the customary course of Ottoman craft customs. He was apprenticed to a recognized master of the guild who had full disciplinary power over him. The apprentice had to learn his trade from the bottom upwards. The apprentices had their workshop which was at the same time a school (*nakışhane*) and a gallery (*nigârhane*) in which to exhibit their works. An interesting method of exhibition is described by Evliya. During public festivals, when the trade guild paraded in procession, while marching the painters exhibited their paintings on the sides of a litter.

Most of the painters were not self-employed. The Sultan's palace always kept a large staff of calligraphers, painters and

[25] For more details see M.Uğur Derman,''Benzeri olmayan bir sanat albümü Gazneli Mahmud Mecmuası'', *Türkiyemiz*, 14 (October 1974) (includes an English summary).

illuminators. According to Evliya, their workshops were at Aslanhane, a large building in the vicinity of the Seraglio, where upper floors were reserved for the most noteworthy artists.

The preparation of a manuscript book had several stages. First, the author or poet would complete the text. The paper would require special treatment, using white lead, starch salammoniac, gum tragacanth and white of egg. These would be mixed or applied separately. As a result of this treatment the paper would become the firm  polished, cream-toned product known as *aharlı* paper. When the sheets were prepared, they were given to calligraphers. After the calligrapher and the margin drawer had completed their part, the blank pages or spaces left, sometimes between lines, for the insertion of miniatures were handed over to the group of painters, *nakkaşan*. Often old texts prove somewhat ambiguous about the meaning of the word *nakkaş* since the word is used for all decorators and ornamentors, as well as for painters. Sometimes to specify 'painter' in old texts, the writer uses the word *ressam,* the very word still in use in Turkish today to signify 'painter' in the Occidental sense. The group of painters as a rule worked collectively and it was a usual practice for every member of the group to be assigned to different technical processes and stages of the work. Generally, the chief master would leave to his apprentices only the execution of subordinate tasks: i.e. *musavvir* and *şebihnüvis* were portraitists; the *tarrah* would make the preliminary drawings; the *renkzen* was the colourist; the *meclisnüvis* planned the composition and groupings; the *siyahkalem,* which literally means 'black pen', we can assume to have been the draughtsman, and so on. Although the author, the calligrapher and the painter worked separately, sometimes the very nature of the work required that they work closely together, such as was the case with miniatures which incorpo-

28

rated lines of text, colophons, or inscriptions inside the miniature as in the books of genealogies which were long series
of portraits arranged like the Tree of Jesse, depicting all the
great personages from Adam and Eve onwards (Fig. 28).
Very intricate scripts were placed on either side of the genealogical tree. There is an interesting miniature in the *Şehname-i
Mehmet Salis* 'The Book of Mehmet III, [ *TSM H. 1609* ],
where the painter of the album, Nakkaş Hasan, in his self portrait
depicts the author and the calligrapher working simultaneously
in the same room (Fig. 29). The inscription in the colophon
of this miniature is an eulogy to the perfection of Seyyit Nakkaş
Hasan's work comparing him on the same level as the famous
Persian painters, Mani and Behzad. It goes on to say that Hasan had given life to his forms. ''When he paints a wrestler,
one can tremble with fear; when he paints the sun, one can feel
the heat, and when he paints a garden, one can feel the perfume
of the rose...''.

29

30

31

32

Unfortunately, we can not adequately assess his skill, as only four miniatures by his hand have survived, all in the above mentioned album. There are few other miniatures depicting the painter in action. For instance, in a Book of Astrology [ *BN Suppl, turc 242* ] two pages have been divided into fifty-six small squares each depicting a trade. Among them is to be found a *nakkaş* or painter (Fig. 30). An interesting feature of these two pages is that they show the democratic mind of the Ottomans, where, among different trades such as that of the dancer, the tailor, the boatman and the lute player, the Sultan is also depicted, regardless of any hierarchical order. Another miniature of the seventeenth century [ *TSM H. 2162*] depicting a painter in the process of drawing a female figure (Fig. 31), carries the signature of a sixteenth century artist of Persian origin Veli Can. This is a falsification. Unfortunately, it was a general practice to sign a picture using the name of a renowned master, either out of respect for the influence he had imparted or because of the wishes of patrons to possess examples of the work of the great masters. Similarly, a miniature of the late fifteenth century, now in the Freer Gallery of Art in Washington, D.C. [*nr. 32.38*], represents an Ottoman painter busy drawing a portrait (Fig. 32) and carries the signature of Behzad, the famous Persian painter, yet it is without the slightest doubt an Ottoman miniature. It was of course due to the widely-known eulogy "with a brush like that of

Behzad'' that so many Ottoman artists were tempted to sign their paintings after the great master.

Of course, there were also foreign masters in the Ottoman Sultan's Place. For instance a document dated 1557 [ *TSM D. 9612/965*] informs us that at that time there were two workshops in the Palace, one Turkish. *Cemaat-i Rum Nakkaşları,* consisting of 26 painters, their chief master being Kara Mimi; the other the foreign *Cemaat-i Acem Nakkaşları,* consisting of nine artists, seven of them Persian from Tabriz, one a Hungarian, and another a Frank by the name of Kıbtas. Probably, among the Sultans themselves and among other members of the Royal family there were those who could be ranked as painters, since by Turkish tradition the Sultan and his children were instructed in some art or science. There were among the Ottoman Sultans accomplished poets and musicians as well as a goldsmith, a spoon maker, a gardener and a maker of bow strings. Although there is no actual record of a sultan-painter, yet we know that a son-in-law of Sultan Ahmet I, Mustafa Paşa, was nicknamed *Nakkaş,* 'painter'.

## ICONOGRAPHICAL THEMES

The main reason for the liberal patronage which was bestowed upon painters by the Ottoman Sultans was the projection of their reigns into future ages. Hence the art of portraiture and of the compilation of chronicles and annals was highly sophisticated, as the Ottomans were more practical and utilitarian as compared with the rulers of other Islamic countries.

I

Turkish artists have painted a very large number of portraits in miniature of the Sultans and other illustrious personalities. Throughout its history Turkish portraiture *(şibih yazmak* or *tasvir yazmak)* has evolved a formula quite its own for representing the face. Apart from the bold and vigoruos use of colours, faces in Turkish portraits are characterized by half-face profile. However, some examples are rendered *en face* hightlighting the individual traits and mood of the character. In contrast, the Persian painter prefers three-quarter profile. While the portraits of contemporary personages were taken from life, Turkish artists dealing with personages from history resorted either to pure imagination, or to copying the portraits of other painters. Apart from the Sultans and their consorts, learned men and artists were also depicted. Following is a list of various fine portraits of Sultans handed down to: that of Sultan Fatih Mehmet II by Sinan Bey *[TSM H. 2153]* ; the portrait of Süleyman I and the portrait of Selim II by the chief painter of Sultan Süleyman's court, Haydar Reis known as Nigâri *[TSM H. 2134]*. Lokman Hüseyin Aşuri's book *Kiyafet-el-insaniye fi şemail el-Osmaniye,* 'The Book of Physiognomy of the Ottoman Dynasty ,contains twelve portraits ranging from Osman I to Murad III executed by the famous sixteenth century Turkish painter Osman[26]. There exist several copies of these *[TSM H. 1562 H. 1563 H. 1564 R. 1264 and R. 1265 İÜK T. 6087 and T. 6088 BM Add. 7880]* (in this last mentioned additions were made up to the period of Ahmet III). The National Library of Scotland has two portraits of Murad *II [ms.d. 1584]*. The manuscripts already mentioned, the Books of Genealogy, the contents of which usually range from pictures of Adam and Eve to that of the latest Sultan, feature portraits of holy men, sovereigns etc. Books of similar nature are *Silsilename* or *Zübdet-üt Tevarih* 'Cream of Histories' of which several copies extant are :

26 Nurhan Atasoy, "Nakkaş Osman'ın Padişah Portreleri Albümü", *Türkiyemiz,* February 1972 no.6 (includes an English summary). For coloured reproductions of these portraits,see also *The world of Islam* (Edited by Bernard Lewis,) London 1976, pp.288-89.

*[TSM H. 1321 CBC no. 414 and TIEM no. 1973]*27.
Some of these feature miniatures depicting religious scenes, a different category of subjects to which we shall refer later. In this present work four miniatures are reproduced from *TIEM no. 1973* on, pages 53, 54, 55 and 56. The last is a portrait of Sultan Mehmet. I. The other *Silsilenames* are : *[TSM H. 1592 H. 1324 H. 1624 A. 3110 A. 3109].*

Also one should mention in this context the portrait in miniature of Murad III on horseback, the present ownership of which is unknown. Another portrait of a Sultan on horseback is that of Süleyman I in the Bibliothèque Nationale. In the same library, in a manuscript dated 1584, are to be found two portraits of Murad III. Topkapı Palace Museum has portraits of Mehmet III, of Ahmet I, Osman II, Murad IV, Mustafa II, Ahmet III, Mahmut I and of Osman III, all executed by Levni who also painted portraits of several personnages of note *[TSM A. 3109].* The National Library of Cairo has a manuscript on the history of Ottoman Sultans by Raşit Efendi which contains 10 portraits *[Hist. turque M. no 30].* Some other portrait albums of later period have been referred to earlier in this book. Apart from the portraits of the Sultans, which are to be found also in the miniatures featured in the Chronicles, their consorts, dignitaries, learned men and artists are also depicted, as in the following examples. There is a portrait of Barbaros Hayrettin Paşa, the famous sixteenth century Turkish admiral painted by Nigâri *[TSM H. 2134].* The Museum of Fine Arts of Boston has a fine portrait of the well-known story-teller La'lin Kaba. A translation of *Şakayik-i Numaniye* 'The Crimson of

27 See Günsel Renda, "The miniatures of Silsilename no.1321 in the Topkapı Saray Museum Library", *Sanat Tarihi Yıllığı*, V, İstanbul 1973,pp. 481-495;G.Renda, "New Light on the Painters of the Zübdet-al Tawarikh in the Museum of Turkish and Islamic Arts in İstanbul", *IVvme Congrès International d'Art Turc*, Editions de l'Université de Provence 1976, pp. 183-200.

the Peony' *[TSM H. 1263]*, in which 49 miniatures in all are to be viewed, presents to us in portraits attributed to the painter, astrologer and poet, Ahmet Nakşi, various Turkish scholars, theologians and artists. Included among them is a portrait of Sultan Mehmet II with his astrologer Ali Kuşçu. Also featured is the well-known Turkish non-conformist thinker of the fifteenth century Şeyh Bedreddin of Simavna, who is seen behind the bars of the prison where he lay awaiting execution in 1420 (Fig. 33). Another manuscript of the same name carries 5 miniatures *[BN Suppl. turc. 1055]*. Finally there is a self-portrait of Ahmet Nakşi himself ,assuming that the miniatures are by his hand. A *tezkiret-üş-şuara* 'Dictionary of the Poets', a biographical dictionary of the poets by Aşık Çelebi, 16th century poet and biographer, contains 74 portraits of illustrious poets *[İstanbul Millet Library Ali Emiri Nr. 772]*. In the last two mentioned some of the miniatures therein are painted from the imagination, and the faces are stereotyped. An interesting miniature by Nakkaş Osman *[TSM A. 3595]* depicts a gathering of illustrious learned men together with calligraphers and painters.

33

II

Painters were required by their royal patrons to portray battle scenes, scenes of enthronement, scenes witnessing the generosity of Sultans, hunting and sportive scenes; and sometimes even scenes celebrating their funerals. As a result, a large number of their miniatures are in the nature of historiography and annals. Artists devoted all their attention to composition and subject matter reproduced in the minutest detail, skilfully combining narrative intent with pictorial realism. They celebrate various incidents of the Sultan's career, including details of his various land campaigns, his naval battles, sieges of enemy fortresses, his hunting expeditions, his sporting interests and several other such displays of strength. We see him galloping across a field or sitting with his chief officers; we are permitted to view his convivial gatherings or his reception of an ambassador. The most important work in this genre is the *Hünername* 'Book of Accomplishments' already referred to. It was supposedly written in four volumes, but only two volumes have survived. The first volume, covering the centuries from the foundation of the Ottoman state to the end of the reign of Selim I, carries 45 miniatures *[TSM H. 1523]* and is dated 1584. The second volume with 65 miniatures is devoted to Sultan Süleyman I's reign *[TSM H. 1524]*. Both volumes are executed by Osman and his workshop. The 23 from both volumes are reproduced in this book.

There are few *Süleymanname* 'Book of Süleyman I', in one of which can be found 69 miniatures spread over the period from the reign of Selim II to that ou Süleyman I *[TSM H. 1517]*. There are three miniatures from this manuscript in this present book on pages 44, 45 and 46. In addition, there is a *Süleymanname* with 25 miniatures *[CBC no. 413]*. Another work from Süleyman I's reign is *Nüzhet el-esrar el-ahbar der sefer-i Sigetvar* 'The History of secret events of the campaign of Sigetvar'. In it there are 20 miniatures *[TSM H. 1339]*. The present book features two of them on pages 47 and 48. *Şehname-i Selim Han* 'The Royal Book of Selim II' covering the period of Selim II's reign contains 43 miniatures *[TSM A. 3595]*, some painted by Osman and some by Ali. Two miniatures from this manuscript are now in the possession of the Boston Museum of Fine Arts. *Selimname* 'The Book of Selim ' *[TSM H. 1597-98,]* with 24 miniatures, is a history in verse illustrated by miniatures done in the same style as the Turkmen school of Shiraz. Another manuscript, bearing the same title but illustrated after the sixteenth century Ottoman style, contains 8 miniatures *[BM Or. 7043]* . *Şehinşahname* 'The Book of the King of Kings', is in two volumes and on the subject of Murat III's reign. The first volume has 58 miniatures depicting various events from the reign of Murat III *[İÜK F. 1404]*. The second has 95 miniatures on the same subject, many of them featuring then famous circumcision festival of 1582 *[TSM B. 200]*. Two of the several miniatures are missing from this manuscript are to be found in the Freer Gallery of Art Washington D.C. There is a manuscript on Ferhat Paşa's conquest of Gence in 1558 called *Kitab-ı Gencine-i Feth-i Gence* with 20 miniatures *[TSM R. 1296]*. *Şecâatname* 'The Book of Courage' on the war waged on Persia by Özdemiroğlu Osman Paşa in 1578-83 contains 77 miniatures *[İÜK T. 6043]*. A manuscript describing the conquest of Georgia, Azerbaijan, and Şirvan by the commander-in-chief Lala Mustafa Paşa exists under the title of *Nusretname* 'The Book of Glory' and carries 41 miniatures *[TSM H. 1365]*. On page 57 is shown, a miniature from this manuscript where above, the historian Mustafa Ali is presenting his book to Lala Mustafa Paşa, and below are whirling dervishes in their ritual dance. A second copy of *Nusretname*, in which eleven miniatures are to be seen, is also extant *[BM Add. 22011]*. A *Şehname* telling of the war with the Hungarians and the capture of Eger during the reign of Murat III, has 4 miniatures executed by Hasan Nakkaş *[TSM H. 1609]*. The poet Nadiri's *Divan*, with 9 miniatures, depicts scenes from the daily life of the Sultans *[TSM H. 889]*. An epic poem, relating to the military expedition of Sinan Paşa to Arabia and Tunisia during the reign of Selim II, *Tarih-Feth-i Yemen* 'History of the Conquest of Yemen' bears 104 miniatures *[İÜK T. 6045]*. An Ottoman history from the foundation of the dynasty to Selim I's reign, *Tacü't Tevarih* 'The Crown of Histories' exists in several illuminated copies, and the miniatures therein mostly are portraits

*[İÜK T. 5970 TSM R. 1112 Paris, Jacquemart-André collection No. INV. I. 1314].* Another book of history is a *Şehname* which has 4 miniatures *[TİEM no. 1965]* A *Paşaname,* 'The Book of the Pasha', describing the military operations of Kenan Paşa against rebels and pirates in Rumeli and on the Black Sea during Murat IV's reign, is illustrated by 6 miniatures *[BM Solane add. 3584].* Last but not least in this category, we can include the *Surnames* or Books of Festivals. There are countless numbers of these manuscripts which relate the progress of various Ottoman Festivals,[28] describing all their splendour and grandeur, however only three of them are illustrated. The first of these is *Surname-i Hümayun,* 'The Imperial Book of Festival', depicting the 1582 festival for the circumcision of Murat III's son, Mehmet III, which lasted more than fifty days and nights, carries 437 miniatures by painter Osman and his workshop. On pages 48, 50, 51 and 52, the present book fetures four of them. Similar representation of the same scenes can be found in the second volume of the *Şehinşahname [TSM B. 200],* already referred to. Probably, there were more miniatures in it but some have been lost. There are a great number of accounts both in Turkish and other languages of the same festival[29]. The other two *surnames* already mentioned are by Levni and his workshop, depicting the festival on the occasion of the circumcision of the four sons of Ahmet III in 1720 *[TSM A. 3593 and A. 3594].* From the former manuscript 9 miniatures are included in the present book on pages 86, 87, 88, 89, 90, 91, 92, 93 and 94. The latter manuscript is less finished and slightly different in style from the former.

### III

Next in popularity to portraiture and chronicles as pro-

28. On these see Metin And, *Kırk Gün Kırk Gece,* İstanbul 1959.

29 For a complete text of a contemporary English account see And, *A History...* pp.118-134.

viding material for illustration were manuscripts of *belles-lettres* and fiction of various kinds. As there was a great reverence for Persian literature, several manuscripts of Persian literature, either in the original or in Turkish translation, were illustrated by Turkish artists. Extant are innumerable illustrated epic, the *Shahname* (or *Şehname)* 'The Book of the King' by Firdowsi's, some by Persian artists and some by Turkish. Here are some examples or the rendefring of Firdowsi's *Şehname* by Turkish artists: *[TSM H. 116 H. 1499 R. 1549 H. 1520 R. 1542 H. 1522 H. 1518 H. 1486 İÜK T. 1631-33 BM Or. 7204 New York Collection of Edwin Binney no. 17 New York Spencer Collection R. 300 BN Suppl. turc 326 Uppsala University Library Coll. Celsing no. 1].* Altogether a total of six hundred miniatures. The title *Şehname* has also been used for chronicles devoted to the achievements of a single Turkish Sultan, some examples of which have already been given.

Illustrated manuscripts of poems fall into three categories: *divan, mesnevi* and anthologies. *Divan* is a volume of the collected works of a poet, grouped and organised according to an established rule. There are several illustrated *divan* manuscripts by either Persian or Turkish poets. For example Fuzuli's *Divan [TSM R. 748 Y. 897 and CBC no. 440],* Selimi's *Divan [İÜK F. 1330],* Khojandi's *Divan [Vienna, Nationalbibliotek Cod. Mixt. 399],* Hidayet's *Divan [CBC no. 401],* Baki's *Divan [TİEM no. 1959 BM Or. 7084 and New York Metropolitan Museum of Art],* Jami's *Divan [TSM H. 987],* Shahi's *Divan [TSM B. 140],* Ulvi Çelebi's *Divan [TSM Halil E. Arda's coll. 34].* Ali Şir Nevai, the great Turkish poet and writer of the fifteenth century of Oriental (Chaghatay) Turkish has left many illustrated manuscripts of Divans *[TİEM no. 1952 under the pseudonym of Fani TSM H. 983 R. 806 R. 804 CBC 409 Cairo Library Lt. Turc no .3].* This present book features three of them in Persian style on pages 33, 34 and 35.

*Mesnevi,* or 'double-rhyme' is a poem in couplets, often hundreds of couplets and occasionally thousands. The subject is usually narrative or didactic. It may be a romance, love stories

34

35

invariably ending unhappily, often a traditional Islamic story, in which case it is usually named after the hero and heroine, for example *Leyla and Majnun.* Or, a *mesnevi* may have religious or mystic content, or may combine mysticism and romance. Mevlana Jalal al-din Rumi's well known *Mesnevi-yi Ma'nevi* has two illustrated manuscripts [*İstanbul Bayazid Library no. 4380 and BM Or. 1963*] . Among several other illustrated *mesnevi* manuscripts we can cite the following: Arifi's *Guy u Çevgân* 'Ball and Polo-stick' [*TSM. H 845*], Fuzuli's *Leyla and Majnun* [*BN Suppl turc. 316 BM Or. 504*], Shaykhi's *Khosrow and Shirin* [*BM Or. 2708 TİEM no. 1960 TSM H. 683 Uppsala University Library no. Vet. 86*], Yahya Beg's *Kitab-ı Şah u Geda* 'The Book of the King and the Beggar [*'New York Collection of Edwin Binney no. 20*], Nev'i Yahya's *Münazara-i tuti ve zagh* 'The Contention of the Parrot and the Crow' [*Berlin Staatsbibliothek Or. Oct. 2121*], Hamdullah Çelebi's *Yusuf and Züleyha* [*CBC no. 428 BM Or. 7111 John Rylands Library at Manchester T. 61 and New York H. P. Kraus Coll. 219-23*], Jami's *Tuhfat al-ahrar* 'Gift for the Free' [*TSM R. 914*], Revani's *İşretname* 'Book of Wassail' *Berlin Staatsbibliothek Or. Oct. 3366*],

Hatifi's *Khosraw and Shirin* *[TSM H. 686 and New York Metropolitan Museum of Art no. 69-27],* Musa Abdi's *Jamaspname [BM Add. 24962],* Assar's *Mihr and Mushtari' Sun and Jupiter' [TSM R. 1027],* Ahmedi's *İskendername' 'Book of Alexander' [BN Colbert 4187].*

A *hamse* 'quintet' is a seris of five *mesnevis.* Ali Şir Nevai's *Hamse* is composed in five *mesnevis* in the following order: *Hayret-i Ebrar* 'The Amazement of the Just', *Ferhad and Şirin, Leyla and Majnun, Seba-i Seyyare* 'The Seven Planets', and the *İskendername. [TSM H. 802].* There exist several illustrated manuscripts of Nizami's *Hamse,* namely: *[TSM R. 871 H. 753 No. 1115 H. 757 B. 145 H. 764],* Jami's *Hamse [CBC no. 166],* Amir Khosrau's *Hamse [TSM H. 799]* Atai's *Hamse* (one of the five books of which is not a *mesnevi,* but a *divan [TSM R. 816 TİEM no. 1969],* Jami's *Heft Evreng'* The Seven Thrones' which consists of seven *mesnevis [TSM N. 805 and B. 143]).*

Of several illustrated manuscripts of anthologies or collections of poems we can cite the following: *[BM Or. 4129 TİEM no. 1968 TSM R. 989 TSM H. 889 H. 1711 CBC no. 424]* and Hoca Sadeddin's *Zübdet el eş'ar* 'Cream of Poems' *[TSM R. 814].*

Some miniatures are anecdotic individually and independently, nothing much matters besides the story it tells in one single miniature, as in books of fables. Some are stories, linking events and episodes like a novel. Some are stories told in prose like Feramzers' *Kıssa-i Şehr'-i Şâtıran* which contains 64 miniatures *[İÜK T. 9303]* and by the same author there is *The Romance of Farruhkhruz* with 64 miniatures *[BM Or. 3298].* An epic novel Şerif's *Destan-ı Faruk and Huma* of the sixteenth century contains 34 miniatures *[İÜK T. 1975],* Lamii's *Şeref ül İnsan'* The Noblesse of Humanity' an ethical prose romance contains 26 miniatures *[BM Add. 7843].*

By the same author, İbret-numa 'Examplar' is a collection of fantastic allegories which contains 8 miniatures [Berlin, Staatsbibliothek Landberg 827]. Attar's well known allegorical poem Mantık al-tair, 'The Conference of the Birds' contains 16 miniatures [TSM E. H. 1512], another illustrated copy of the same work contains 3 miniatures [New York Collection of Edwin Binney no. 1]. Husein Vaiz Kashifi's ethical treatise Ahlak-ı Muhsini contains 2 miniatures [TSM R. 392]. Illustrated manuscripts of fables designed to educate in an entertaining way are also extant. For instance, there is Kelile and Dimne, a famous collection of animal fables of Indian origin to be found in Bombay's Prince of Wales Museum [Ms. 51.34] with seven miniatures, and another damaged copy with 4 miniatures [BM Or. 7354]. Ali B. Salih's Hümayunname 'Imperial Book' (it is called thus because it is believed to have didactic value for the conduct and decisions of rulers), is a translation of the Persian Husein Vaiz Kashifi's Envar-i Süheyli 'Lights of Canopus' which is an ornate re-telling of the Indian fables of Bidpay, in which the miniatures are endowed with a sense of humour. One copy of this carries 165 miniatures [BM Add. 15153] and the other 88 miniatures [TSM R.] translation of the Persian Husein Vaiz Kashifi's Envar-i Süheyli 'Lights of Canopus' which is an ornate re-telling of the Indian fables of Bidpay, in which the miniatures are endowed with a sense of humour. One cop iyof this carries 165 miniatures [BM Add. 15153] and the other 88 miniatures [TSM R. 843] . Sometimes a single miniature can be found inserted among a series on a different subject. For instance in [İÜK T. 6043] there is miniature depicting a fable of Mevlana on cats and parrots. Likewise the same manuscript contains another miniature depicting a lion and a jackal, probably illustrating another fable.

Ottoman miniature painting lembraces a vast range of Moslem religious thought and mythology. Illustrations of sacred stories, however, are seldom designed to assist the mood of devotion. It is evident that those works are not paralleled as a whole by any known example of Persian or any other Islamic miniature painting. A monumental example of this type of work is *Siyer-i Nebi* 'The Acts of the Prophet' by Mustafa Darir in six volumes, only five of which have survived, dispersed throughout several different collections. The first, second and sixth volumes are in Topkapı Palace Museum *[TSM H. 1221-23].* They contain a total of 349 miniatures. The third volume is in New York Public Library's Spencer Collection and comprises 128 miniatures, while the fourth volume in the Chester Beatty Collection in Dublin *[No. 419]* has 136 miniatures. The National Library in Dresden possesses some of those fragments of *Siyer-i Nebi* believed to be from the fifth volume. Another copy of *Siyer-i Nebi* by Darir, though not from the 6 volume set, contains 193 miniatures *[TİEM no. 1974].* A document exists which states clearly that the six volumes contained a total of 814 miniatures. The five extant volumes totalling 613 miniatures which means that the missing volume should have contained 201 miniatures. These illustrations, mostly of a sacred nature, not only depict scenes from the life of the Prophet and of members of his family, of his

 36
 37

companions and of the saints with attendant references to miracles, mysteries and angels, but also scenes on Biblical themes, taken from Old and New Testament stories. A distinct system of iconography was invented and some conventions and symbols are employed in the compositions such as a pear-shaped flaming halo representing the Prophet. At other times the Prophet is represented simply by a flame such as the case in Fig. 34 *[CBC no. 414]*, where the Prophet is mounted on Buraq, the steed of Paradise, on his heavenward flight, or, if he has a face, freguently it is hidden by a veil hanging from the forehead to the chin.[30] Another convention is Ali's two-pointed sword. The clothing of Jesus belongs to a world of Ottoman rather than Christian thought. Here (Fig.28) *[Vienna, Nationalbibliothek A.F. 50]* depicts Jesus portrait (lower figure on the left) in a Tree of Jesse. The others being Alexander the Great, the upper figure on the left, Zacharias on the right, and St. John the Baptist on the lower right. The other (Fig. 35) *[IÜK T. 6624]* is the descent of Jesus with the help of angels on a minaret in Damascus, yet another (Fig. 36) *[IÜK T. 6624]* depicts Jesus leading an army. In all three Jesus is depicted in Ottoman attire. And (Fig. 37) *[TSM H. 1703]* depicts the Virgin Mary holding one of her breasts to suckle the baby Jesus.

In this vein Huseyn Vaiz Kashifi's *Rawzat ush-Shuhada* [31]

30 On rare occasions some of the ordinary people's faces are omitted. An amusing example of this occurs in one of the manuscripts [CBC no.444],in which roses are substituted for faces in view of the Islamic prohibition of representing God's creatures and thus, the faces of all human beings, and even a horse's head cannot be depicted. See V. Minorsky's *The Chester Beatty Library. A Catalogue of the Turkish Manuscripts and Miniatures,* Dublin 1958,p.81.

31 Not to be confused with *Rawzat al-Safa* 'Gardenof Purity' by Mir Khvand,a history book depicting all that had happened in the world since the Creation of which there is an an illustrated manuscript with 11 miniatures [BM Or. 5736]. See G.M. Meredith - Owens," A Copy Rawzat al-Safa with Turkish Miniatures", *Paintings from Islamic Lands,* (Edited by R. Pinder-Wilson), Oxford 1969, pp.110-123.

'Garden of Martyrs' which deals chiefly with the suffering and martyrdoms of the Imams Hasan and Huseyn, the grand-sons of the Prophet, has an illustrated manuscript with 12 miniatures *[Berlin Staatsbibliothek Diez A. ol 5.]* Fuzuli, the great Turkish poet wrote a history of the Holy Family of Islam, a free adaptation of the Kashifi's work which he called *Hadikat üs Sü'ada* 'The Garth of the Blessed' though it comprises of many details from other sources which there are countless illustrated manuscripts, namely *[BM Or 7301 Or. 12009 TİEM no.* 1967 *İstanbul Süleymaniye Library Fatih 4321 Konya Mevlana Museum no.4 and Hemdam Çelebi vakfı no. 101 New York Collection of Edwin Binney no.4 New York Brooklyn Museum no. 70-143 BN Suppl. turc 1088 and Ankara Ethnographical Museum].* Lamii Çelebi's *Maktel-i Âl-i Resul* or *Maktel-i Imam Huseyn,* poems on the martyrdom of Imam Huseyn *[BM Or. 7238]* contains 7 miniatures, while *TİEM no. 1958* has 8 miniatures, Jami's *Nafahat al-uns* 'The Breaths of İntimacy' on the biographies of the saints *[CBC no. 474]* has miniatures. Fig. 38 depicts the martyrdom of Mansur al-Hallaj from this manuscript. Some miniatures were done to illustrate manuscripts on holy per-sonnages, sufis, ascetics and the like, or books of divination. Suhraverdi's book *Jami al-siyer* 'The collector of Sacred Acts' on the history of prophets, caliphs and saintly people, has two illustrated volumes. Volume I *[TSM H. 1369]* has 6 miniatures and volume II *[TSM H. 1230]* 9 miniatures. The reproduction on page 84 depicting the encounter of Mevlana Jalal al din Rumi with and Molla Shems al-din is from volume II. Likewise *Menakib-i Hazret-i Mevlana* (or *Menakab-i Tavakib)* 'The Acts of Mevlana' by Mahmut Dede depicting the life of the famous mystic poet Mevlana Jalal al-din Rumi, has two illustrated manuscripts. The first one bears 22 miniatures *[TSM R. 1479]* and the second *[New York Morgan Library no.M 466]* has 29 miniatures. The miniatures on pages 79,80,81 82 and 83 of this book are from *TSM R. 1479 Falname* 'The

Book of Divination *[TSM H. 1703].* bears 35 miniatures, some portraying scenes featuring various prophets. The present book on page 84 depicts the expulsion of Adam and Eve from Paradise. Similarly Kazvini's well-known book, *Acaib el Mahlukat ve garaib el mevcudat* 'The Marvels and Peculiarities of the is Creation' a cosmographical work of which several copies either in shortened translation or unabridged exist : *[Cairo Bibliothèque Egyptienne Hist. Turque M.no 125 TSM H. 408 A. 3632 R. 1662 R. 1088 H. 409 BM Add. 7894 BN Suppl. Turc 1063].* It is noticeable in this work that some of them miniatures manifest a pseudo-sacred character.

V  38

In such works of art the landscape, and views generally speaking, are treated as decoration and background. The drawing of the trees is distinctive, the forms of foliage and the colour used in painting them produce a subtle decorative effect. Landscape in its most varied forms was a favourite setting especially when illustrating manuscripts of poetry (see for instance pages 33, 34 and 35). However, in the anthology of Persian poems *[TIEM no. 1950],* we have a unique example of the art of pure use of landscape. This unique work which has aroused the interest of many students is adorned with twelve miniatures. Scholars have been puzzled by its provenance as it does not fit with any previously known Persian example, though the text is Persian and the artistry is very different from Turkish painting. Yet one scholar, Ivan Stchoukine, has produced strong evidence in defence of the point of view that the miniatures in this work are the work of Turkish artists [32] If he is right in assigning them to Turkish artists, these are very

32 See Ivan Stchoukine, "Origine turque des peintures d'une anthollogie persane de 801/1398", *Syria,* 42 (1965), pp.137-140.

reminiscent of the filograms already referred to. They are empty of animal or human figures except for one which depicts several birds such as wild geese, sparrows and magpies. Delicate veining of the leaves, blossoming trees, vines and serpentine plants are crowded in to give the effect of dense foliage; together with steeply-rising mountains, a small lake and stylized grasses, these produce a landscape rich in pattern.

A Turkish artist already referred to in this text, Matrakçı Nasuh [33], evolved a different style of miniature painting in which landscape is combined with topographical designs. In his work, the important buildings of a city together with its walls, its fortresses and its houses, and the brooks, lakes, rivers and mountains of the surrounding countryside are seen from above in a map-like perspective. The whole is viewed from different angles: while the city within its confines is seen from above, the architectural setting is simultaneously viewed from side elevations and from the front. Nasuh could record his visual observations and interpret nature and towns most effectively. As a matter of fact in the text he states clearly "...I have written and painted all the places, cities, towns, villages, fortresses, giving their names and pictures." The artist has all but dispensed with human elements in his composition. Yet, he is far from being dry in his rendering of the topographical layout. The artist has sought to inject human interest by including deers, birds, fishes, rabbits, ducks and swans, many of which have received sympathetic treatment of expression, though in the eight colour reproductions in the present book there is no animals, except in the one on page 40. Conventionalised grasses, slender cypresses, ponds, brooks and rivers are also featured lovingly by this master colourist. Matrakçı has left

33 On Matrakçı Nasuh one should consult two studies by Professor Hüseyin Yurdaydın, *Matrakçı Nasuh,* Ankara 1963 and "Two new Illuminative works of Matrakçı Nasuh", *Atti del Secondo Congresso Internazionale di Arte Turca,* Napoli 1965, pp.283-286.

three illustrated manuscripts in this same style. The first is *Beyan-ı Menazil-i Sefer-i Irakeyn* 'An account of each stage of the campaign in the two Iraqs' (both Arab and Persian), better known as *Mecmua-i Menazil* 'Itineraries' *[İÜK T 5969]*, which has 132 miniatures, depicting each stops visited on the army's routes. Eighty two of these miniatures depict inhabited buildings and towns, and of these cities 47 are within the present boundaries of Turkey, 20 are in Iran and finally 15 are in the Tigris and Euphrates region of Iraq. The present book presents eigth of these miniatures in the following order: İstanbul (p.36), Erzurum (p. 37), Eskişehir (p.38), Diyarbakır formerly Kara Amid (p. 39), Sultaniye,Northwest Iran (p.40), Han-ı Beriz, east of Baghdad (p.41), Bitlis (p.42), and Kasaba-i Derguzin, North of Hamadan in Iran (p.43).

The second manuscript is the *Süleymanname* 'The Book of Süleyman I' *[TSM H. 1608]*, with 32 miniatures divided into two sections. The first part depicts High Admiral Barbaros Hayrettin's visit to France in 1543, incorporating visits by the fleet to such Mediteranean ports as Antibes, Nice, Toulon, Genoa, and Reggio. The second part is an account of Süleyman's expedition against Austria for control of Hungary. From this manuscript (Fig. 39) depicts Estergon and (Fig. 40) the fortress of Tata.

The third work of Nasuh is *Tarih-i Sultan Beyazid* 'The History of Sultan Beyazid II' *[TSM R. 1272]* containing ten miniatures depicting various cities and fortresses such as Kili, Akkerman, İnebahtı, Avarna, Moton and Gülek. Also featured is the Ottoman fleet of this period (Fig. 41).

39          40          41

Similar features can be detected in some of the fine examples of Ottoman cartography. For instance, the *Kitab-i Bahriye* 'Book of Navigation' by the well-known Turkish navigator and cartographer Piri Reis *[TSM H. 642 and R. 1633]* develops along these lines. It is in two volumes, the first having 215 and the second 223 maps which bear the date 1525-26. Some of these maps depict Mediaterrnean ports, as in Nasuh's work. Incidentally Piri Reis' map of the world made in 1513 shows the American continent. Photographs recently taken from space of the coastlines he drew have given rise to great speculation about his amazing accuracy. A book called *Hadis-i Nev veya Tarihi Hind-i Garbi,* 'A new Event or the History of the West Indies,' contains fourteen miniatures depicting the natives and animals of the newly-discovered American continent, and two maps. A complimentary copy was presented to Sultan Murad III *[TSM R. 1488].* It exists in another copy with 3 miniatures *[İstanbul Beyazid Library no. 4969].*

In this vein there are a great number of single miniatures inserted in the manuscripts containing miniatures of different categories. For instance, a two-page spread depicting the city of Manisa *[TSM A. 3592].* Another miniature depicting Kars around the years 1580 *[İÜK F. 1404]* and Fig. 42 also depicts the rebuilding of Kars and repairing of the fortifications, after it was taken by the Ottoman towards the end of the 16th century *[BM Add. 1582].* Yet another copy exists of the latter *[TSM H. 1365].* Both miniatures gives much information on Kars in its details. Likewise in a manuscript *[İÜK T. 6624]* out of 59 miniatures we find one which depicts At Meydanı in İstanbul, the ancient Byzantine Hippodrome, including the mosque of St Sophia. Fig. 43 is an accurate rendering of the Mosque of Süleymaniye in İstanbul *[CBC no. 413].* In the same manuscript we find a miniature depicting a stylized rendering of the forts of Szigetvar. Fig. 44 also 42

depicts Szigetvar almost in the same style as Matrakçı Nasuh
[TSM H. 1339]. There exist also several imaginary renderings
of cities. For example in a manuscript [CBC no. 444] we
find two of İstanbul and two of Aleppo, all depicted by imagination, besides a European landscape, the Nile, Mecca and
Medina. The last mentioned favourite and sacred subjects
were very common. Several miniatures exist depicting Mecca,
Medina and the Kaaba, Muhammed's tomb, and other sanc-
tuaries, namely CBC no. 447 and no. 443 TSM Y. 141.
Of more recent times there is a manuscript depicting 30 towns

43        44

already referred to, and two examples from this are reproduced
in Fig. 25 and Fig. 26.

## VI

There is another category of iconographical subject matter
which is concerned with the reality and conditions of everyday
life. It was compiled without any religious or historical signi-
ficance. Hence it provides a visual record of a social order which
has passed away, and, as such, these paintings are valuable
and are precious testimony to Turkish concepts of life. They
tell us what types of clothes were worn by the people, what
type of entertainment prevailed and in what type of habitation
the people lived, and so on. Usually *murakkas*, albums containing

collections of a variety of subjects, - often executed by different hands in different periods, - contain a large amount of material of this category. The best examples are from the so-called album of Ahmet I *[TSM B. 408]* and the albums *[TSM H. 2155 and H. 2148]* also show among other things, clown dancers, various people in costume, a men's public bath (Fig. 4) *[TSM B. 408]*, the sojourn of a caravan on its journey, a wedding scene, and two lovers caught at night in a surprise raid by the police. The former album heralds Levni's style more than a century previous to his emergence. One need only compare this work with Levni's miniature depicting a notable carried in a palanquin *[TSM H. 2155]*. Another *murakka* in Dublin *[CBC no. 439]* is typical of this category, especially one particular miniature, the most noticeable, featuring a coffee house with forty-seven people engaged in a variety of different pastimes (Fig. 45).

As already stressed, the Sultan's interest in and influence on the evolution of art and taste resulted in miniature painting being closely connected with to the court. Most of the surviving examples come from this source. However, some examples from outside the court have been handed down to us. They reflect a local folk culture and a popular taste closely associated with the needs of the market and were produced by artisans and small shopkeepers. Probably these miniatures, done in a very naive and primitive fashion, where artists have not troubled to produce finished work, are strongly caricaturized. Although the execution rarely attains the perfection of the court artists they are not without certain charm. Colour plays a less important role, for they are really only a tinted drawings. The best example of this popular type is an anonymous album of the seventeenth century, once in the possession of the late Professor Franz Taeschner but destroyed in the Second World War. Before destruction it was fortunately printed in monochrome with

a few coloured reproductions[34]. Another volume, probably a companion to the first one, is now in Venice *[Museu Civivo Correr. Ms. Cigone 1971]*[35]. It features a very precise record of local events involving a wide choice of subjects. Among them are naval battles, buildings, entertainments, fires *(Fig. 46)*, punishments, social gatherings, sailing-boats (Fig. 47) and even a portrait of the Sultan. A third volume, also

46 47

of the seventeenth century, is now in the Kungliga Biblioteket in Stockholm. It has not however been inspected by the present author. A large number of albums of this kind, mostly depicting various costumes of functionaries and people of different social rank and profession are dispersed throughout a number of collections. The British Museum has several albums of this type including *[Sloane 5258 (263), Add 23880; 22367]*. Three albums dating from the seventeenth century are housed in the Bibliothèque Nationale in the Départment des Estampes *[Od. 6-8]*. The first of these contains 49 miniatures and was published in black and white by Professor Süheyl Ünver in 1958. Here (Fig. 7) depicting the young lover with a lute serenading his beloved who is looking from the window and

34 Franz Taeschner, *Alt-Stambuler Hof.Und Volksleben. Ein Türkisches Miniaturenalbum aus dem XVII Jahrhundert,* Hannover 1925 (contains 4 color and 51 monochromed reproductions).

35 See Metin And, "XVII yüzyılda bir halk ressamı", *Tarih Mecmuası,* november 1970 no.10.

(Fig. 48) depicting a woman playing a rebeck are from these albums. A similar album of the seventeenth century with 100 miniatures is in Warsaw, Biblioteka Narodowa *[Cod BOZ 165]*. Similar types of miniatures to be found in the Riiksmuseum voor Volkenkunde in Leiden in an eighteenth century album. From this album (Fig. 49) represents Ağa Çuhadarı, one of the Sultan's attendants. The Österrechische National Bibliothek in Vienna possesses seven volumes of albums dating from the seventeenth and eighteenth centuries *[Cod. 8562-64; 8574; 8602-04]* which contain hundreds of miniatures of Turkish costumes with captions in Italian. Although they are catalogued under 'occidental illuminated manuscripts',

48    49

it is the present writer's opinion that they were executed by Turkish artists, as they are very much in the same style as the albums referred to above.

VII

Lastly, scientific texts where greatly helped by miniatures: books on cosmology, cosmography, geography, on natural history, on mathematics, astronomy and astrology, physics and especially on mechanical devices, on medicine and pharmacology, on alchemy, on various occult cryptic sciences, including cabbalistic formulaes, revelations and prophecies concerning the end of the world, and on man in the cosmic order. Some illustrations in are the form of miniature painting, and some are in the form of diagrams, that is, drawings explanatory in purpose, in which all elements are represented with scientific clarity and simplification. Manuscripts on astrology, cosmography, divination and magic have been handed down to us from those times as there was a courtly concern in these matters. Some are manuscripts where the content of the text is not concerned with these subjects, but in them we find such miniatures having purely a scientific or technical interest. For instance, the miniature on page 53, in which the structure of the macrocosmos is depicted, in which the whole cosmos is drawn distinct and mapped within: the earth surrounded by seven concentric skies each in a different colour and corresponding to one of the prophets; the zodiacal signs; phases of the moon illustrated by circular figures divided into 28 mansions according to the days of the months and indicating the hour of the night at which the moon rises with 28 hireatic symbols corresponding, and finally beyond the visible and tangible world the realms of angels, the cosmos represented by angels in the four quarters of the universe. Other examples of this category are two miniatures from Şehinşahname [İÜK F. 1404] one depicting a giant armillary sphere where one astronomer is adjusting the meridian rings while three other astronomers are taking observations. Another interesting point in this miniature is the correct rendering of perspective and foreshortening. The other miniature from the same manuscript depicts the chief astrologer Takiyüddin in his observatory working with other astronomers. The miniature is full of instruments such as an astrolabe, an alidade attached to a quadrant, a diopter, rhumbs, globes, an hourglass and others, and the correct handling of some of these instruments is shown in the hands of the astronomers. Another miniature of similar vein depicts an astronomer observing with a quadrant a comet flying over İstanbul in 1577 (Fig.50), the same scene is depicted in other miniatures, namely *[İÜK T. 6043]* and *[CBC no. 444]*.

Some miniatures show the constellations of the zodiac, with fixed stars rendered either in schematic and diagramatic compositions, or personified and allegorical renderings in the shape of animals, birds and human figures. For these the best example is the manuscript *[TSM B. 274]* with 45 miniatures, the original of it being *[İÜK T. 5953]* also with 45 miniatures, where a suggestion of modelling, a sense of relief and roundness is present, as is the case in Fig. 51. Already referred to are the treatises on geography and the maps containing miniatures

50  51  52

some with figural illustrations. One interesting example of this kind ise book of maps of  which the date of production, the place and the artist are unknown, but it was definitely prepared by a Turkish artist though not Ottoman, *[TSM B.334];* it contains several maps ornamented with peacocks,  nude mermaids, angels, a man picking dates, Jonah coming out of the whale, fishes, trees, a lion grasping a man by his clothes, and so on

Similarly albums featuring pictures of galleys and boats *[TSM R. 1192 and H. 1627]* and other with pictures of musical instruments *[TSM H. 1793]* should also be mentioned. There are also books of magical signs, featuring demoniac,

fantastic animals and evil figures. The painting of some of them is often very crude but they have considerable importance from the iconographical point of view. One where it is believed most of the numerous minatures are by Osman's workshop is *BN suppl, turc 242. Davetname* 'The Book of Summons', that is, summoning spirits *[İAK T. 208]* is another example of this and contain 34 miniatures with some diagrams depicting creatures with several heads, or half beasts half human. (See Fig. 52). Yet another book on divination is *TSM B. 373*.

Some painters seem to have had a passion for birds and other animals, as though the text might have been written for animal fables, and they are anecdotic illustrations as we have already pointed out, yet they are interesting for the study of natural history and zoology. A manuscript *[BM Harleian 5500]* without title and author's name, dealing with the wonders of art and nature contains 90 miniatures. (Fig. 53) from this manuscript depicts a pelican or an adjutant stork from India, which, during a season of drought when similar birds are on the point of perishing from lack of water, dispenses water from its capacious crop to these others as an act of charity. There are also some individual drawings in albums which show a certain verisimilitude in the scientific manner of their texture and their anatomy, such as the birds of prey in *[TSM H. 2133]*, the woodcock in *[TSM H. 2155]*, the magpie in *[TSM H. 2162]* and others. Also painters imagined a number of fabulous beasts which seem credible however fantastic, such as a creature which is a composite figure made up of parts from various animals, and was believed to make its appearance on the Last Day or The Day of Judgement. There are two versions of this belonging to two copies of the same manuscript. The first *[İÜK T. 6624]* depicts this animal with the head of a stag, the ears of an elephant, the legs and neck of a camel, the wings of a bird, and human arms and hands and holding a wand with an animal head. The second version of it *[TSM B. 373]* has slight modifications, and the animal resembles more a unicorn with a human face.

The plants, flowers and trees in the miniatures have a purely decorative fashion or rarely a symbolic function. Yet painters especially from the 17th century onwards revealed a greater sensitivity to flowers and fruits according to some preconceived scheme of purely decorative content like a still-life painting. A manuscript of poems *[İÜK T. 5650]* contains 34 miniatures of various flowers. Another manuscript *[TSM H. 912]* of poems selected from Sultan Selim III's poetry contains eleven miniatures; apart from two landscapes and one depicting the rose, the others are studies of various fruits such as grapes, pears, pomegranates, peaches. An interesting manuscript of poems is entitled *Sümbülname* 'The Book of the Hyacinth' *[TSM H. 413]* where forty, pages of the text are illustrated with hyacinths. We have already referred to an album *[İÜK T. 5461]* which, among other subjects contains several miniatures and filograms depicting flowers in a vase and fruits. Some of these painting belong to the realm of the abstract and their intrinsic beauty of growth, color and texture are formal and patternized such as the flower and stylised leaves in *[TSM H. 2163]*, yet some are scientifically perfect as botanical recordings.

For medical and surgical treatises the best example already referred to is *Cerrahiye el-haniye* by Sabuncuoğlu of which there are three copies extant *[BN Suppl turc 963-İstanbul Fatih Millet Library no. 79 and İstanbul Faculty of Medicine Library of the Institute of History of Medicine T. Y. 263].* The original and most complete of the three manuscripts is the BN copy of it, which contains 136 miniatures on the treatment of illnesses and operations such as Caesarean operation, cauterization, treatment of disclocated parts, dentistry, treatment of haemorrhoids and other such scenes where, besides the scientific interest, a playful grotesqueness pleases the artist's fancy (see Fig. 22 and Fig. 23). In addition there are 18 illustrations of surgical instruments.

# CONCLUSION

The present survey is, of necessity, an abbreviated one, involving in consequence drastic over-simplification. But even this broad outline stresses the fact that it was high time a serious appraisal of Turkish miniature painting was made. Turkish miniature painting is like other Oriental arts in that it has a perceptible effect on contemporary taste. The artists represent reality more really than a picture based on projective geometry. They do not view nature with an innocent eye but seek to discover an unexpected alternative. As it turns out the perspective they arrived at rather fits the approach of contemporary modern painting. Further, the modern Turkish artist, trying to find a modern Turkish alternative to a culture directly inspired by the West, has been aided by the fact that the techniques and styles of Turkish traditional artistic creation are already fairly modern. A still life by Braque, in which some of the fruits which form the subject overlap the borderline of his painting, finds a rich antecedent in buildings which often project out of the frame of the miniature.

Although the scholarly study of Turkish minliture painting evolved relatively recently, a group of young Turkish scholars, among whom are Nurhan Atasoy, Esin Atıl, Filiz Çağman, Günsel Renda, Güner İnal and Zeren Akalay, with their monographs on historical research of style and iconographical analysis, have blazed a path which will finally lead to complete systematic cataloguing and inventorising of collections. This will be a move towards enlightening the ignorance of European as well as Turkish people who still in the main know little about Turkish miniature art will be seen to have an important role to play in future Turkish studies and will take its place as one of the great achievements of Turkish civilization.

## Bibliographical Notes

For an exhaustive bibliography on Turkish miniature painting see Nurhan Atasoy, **Türk Minyatür Sanatı Bibliyografyası,** İstanbul 1972. For artists' names in different workshops, their payrolls, their works which they created on special occasions to be presented to the Sultan, the lists of material bought by the Court for the use of the artists in 136 documents see Rıfkı Melûl Meriç, **Türk Nakış Sanatı Tarihi Araştırmaları,** Ankara 1953. For two major source books on Ottoman miniature painters, see Mustafa Ali, **Menakib-i Hünerveran,** İstanbul 1926, and Evliya Çelebi, **Seyahatname,** volumes I - X İstanbul 1928. For a shortened English translation see Evliya Efendi. **Narrative of Travels in Europe, Asia and Africa in the Seventeenth Century...,** translated from the Turkish by Ritter Joseph von Hammer, London 1846, vol I, part 2, «The Thirty - sixth Section. The Painters», pp. 217 - 221.

Books in English and in French on Turkish miniature painting: G. M. Meredith-Owens, **Turkish Miniatures,** London 1963; Emel Esin, **Turkish Miniature Painting** Tokyo 1960; Ivan Stchoukine, **La Peinture Turque d'apres Les Manuscrits Illustrés,** Paris, volume I (1966). volume II (1971); K. Yetkin, **L'ancienne peinture Turque du XIIe au XVIIIe siècle,** Paris 1970; R. Ettinghausen. **Turkish Miniatures from the 13th to the 18th Century,** Milano 1965 (UNESCO); Z. V. Togan, **On the Miniatures in İstanbul Libraries,** İstanbul 1963; M.Ş. İbşiroğlu and S. Eyüboğlu, **Turkey - Ancient Miniatures,** New York 1961 (UNESCO World Art Series). Nurhan Atasoy-Filiz Çağman, **Turkish Miniature Painting,** İstanbul 1974. A few chapters in a number of general books on Turkish art, Islamic art or Islamic painting : Sir Thomas Arnold, **Painting in Islam,** Oxford

1928; C. Esat Arseven, **L'Art Turc,** İstanbul 1939; Oktay Aslanapa, **Turkish Art and Architecture,** London 1971; M. Ş. İbşiroğlu, **Das Bild im Islam. Ein Verbot und seine Folgen,** Wien-München 1971; Ernst Kühnel, **Miniaturmalerei im Islamischen Orient,** Berlin 1923; F. R. Martin, **The Miniature Paintings and Painters of Persia, India and Turkey from the 8th to the 18th Century,** 2 vols, London 1912; David Talbot Rice, **Islamic Painting. A Survey,** Edinburgh, 1971.

Catalogues of collections and exhibitions: Fehmi Ethem Karatay - I. Stchoukine, **Les Manuscripts Orientaux Illustrés de la Bibliothéque de l'Université de Stamboul,** Paris 1933; V. Minorsky - J.V.S. Wilkinson, **The Chester Beatty Library, A Catalogue of the Turkish Manuscripts and Miniatures,** Dublin 1958; Filiz Öğütmen, **Miniature Art from the XIIth to the XVIII century** (A Guide to the Miniature Section of Topkapı Saray / İstanbul 1966; **Art Treasures of Turkey, Washington,** D. C., 1966; Ernst J. Grube, **Miniature Islamiche dal XIII al XIX secolo da collezioni amaricane,** Venezia 1962.

## List of Illustrations

The miniatures in the present book are from the following sources: Ali Şir Nevai's *Divan [TSM H. 804 and H. 806]* dating 1434-1540. (The following miniatures are from Ali Şir Nevai's *Divan*: Pages 33, 34 and 35). Matrakçı Nasuh's *Beyan-ı Menazil-i Sefer-i Irakeyn* 'An account of each stage of the campaign in the two Iraqs' dating 1537-38 *[İÜK T. 5964]* (The following miniatures are from this manuscript: pages 36, 37, 38, 39, 40, 41, 42, and 43). Arifi's *Süleymanname* 'The Book of Süleyman I' *[TSM H. 1517]* dating 1558. (The following miniatures are from *Süleymanname*: pages 44, 45 and 46). Ahmet Feridun Paşa's *Nüzhet el esrar el ahbar der sefer-i*

*Szigetvar* 'An account fo secret events on the campaign of Szigetvar' *[TSM H. 1339]* dating 1658-69. (The miniatures on pages 47 and 48). Lokman's *Surname-i Hümayun* 'The Imperial Book of Festival' *[TSM H. 1344]* dating 1582-3. (The following miniatures are from *Surname:* pages 49, 50, 51 and 52). Lokman's *Zübdet-üt-Tevarih* 'Cream of Histories' *[TIEM no. 1972]* dating 1583. (The following miniatures are from *Zübdet-üt-Tevarih:* pages 53, 54, 55 and 56). Mustafa Ali's *Nusratname* 'The Book of Glory' dating 1584./ *[TSM h. 1365]*. (The following miniature from *Nusratname:* page 57). Lokman's *Hünername* 'The Book of Accomplishments' volume I dating 1584 and volume II dating 1588 *[TSM H. 1523 and H. 1524]*. (The following miniatures are from *Hünername:* The Front cover, pages 58, 59, 60, 61, 62, 63, 64, 65, 66, 67, 68, 69, 70, 71, 72, 73, 74, 75, 76, 77, 78 and the Back Cover). Mahmud Dede's *Menakib-i Hazret-i Mevlana* 'The Acts of Mevlana' dating 1599 *[TSM R. 1479]*. (The following miniatures are om *Menakib:* pages 79, 80, 81, 82 and 83). Suhraverdi's *Jami al-siyer* 'The Collector of Sacred Acts' dating around 1600. *[TSM H. 1230]*. (The following miniature is from *Jami al-siyer:* page 84). Kalender Paşa's *Falname* 'The Book of Divination' dating around 1610 *[TSM H. 1703]*. (The following miniature is from *Falname:* page 85). Vehbi's *Surname* 'The Book of Festival' dating around 1720 *[TSM A. 3593]*. (The following miniatures are from *Surname:* pages 86, 87, 88, 89, 90, 91, 92, 93, and 94). The last two miniatures by Levni *[TSM H. 2164]* on pages 95 and 96.

Front Cover: Sultan Orhan Gazi presents his bow which he himself has tried out. Back Cover: A view from Topkapı Palace. The Imperial Gate, the First Court and the Central Court.

p.33. A picnic of a Prince
p.34. A hunting scene.

p.61. Çelebi Sultan Mehmet I on route for the Wallachia campaign, punishing the thieves who have stolen honey from some hives at Rusçuk on the Danube.

p.62. Murad I spears a wolf dressed in armour.

p.63. Beyazid I hunting at Yenişehir, a village near Bursa.

p.64. A falcon escapes from the hand of Murad I on his arrival at the Kaplıca Hospice when returning from the hunt.

p.65. A lion brought by a tamer from Bagdad licks Osman I's boots.

p.66. The death of Mehmet I is concealed from the army.

p.67. The battle of Niğbolu (Nicepolis) on the Danube, between Bayazid I's army and the Crusaders.

p.68. Accession of Beyazid I at Kosova.

p.69. Sultan Orhan Gazi shows his strenght he raises a huge mace and after holding it for a while on his lap, puts it aside.

p.70. A fight in the presence of Bayazid II between a lion presented by the Sultan of Tunisia and a water buffalo, which Bayazid eventually kills.

p.71. Accession of Osman I.

p.72. Murad II shoots three arrows into a target in the presence of an ambassador.

p.73. Sultan Mehmet II the Conqueror casting a mace at the Serpentine Column in the Hippodrome at İstanbul.

p.74. Uğurlu Mehmet Bey, son of Uzun Hasan watches his father's standards in the presence of the Mehmet II.

p.75. The execution of a man who tried to kill Sultan Bayazid II while crossing a river.

p.76. Mehmet II assaulting the fortress of Belgrade.

p.77. The Battle of Mohacs in 1526.

p.78. Soliman I,'the Magnificent' in a hunting party.

p.79. Mevlana Jalal-al-din Rumi standing among his disciples.

p.80. Mevlana Jalal-al-din Rumi sitting among his disciples.

p.81. Mevlana Jalal-al-din Rumi saving a ship caught in a whirlpool.

p.82. A bull paying tribute to Mevlana Jalal-al-din Rumi.

p.83. Mevlana Jalal-al-din Rumi talking to a water creature, while his family stands amazed.

p.84. Mevlana Jalal-al-din Rumi encounters his consecrator Shamsu'l-din of Tabriz.

p.85. The expulsion of Adam and Eve from Paradise (on the right a serpent holds some leaves in its mouth, and an angel dressed in red.

p.86. The barbers' and candle-makers' corporations parading in the Imperial festival. In the foreground some dancing boys and jesters, some with masks and comic hats.

p.87. Sultan Ahmet III watching the procession, behind him stand two princes and the chief eunuch, and on the left in a smaller tent the grand vizir. In the procession a palanquin is carried by two mules.

p.88-90. The two-page spread miniature depicting Sultan Ahmet III watching dancers on water and other water spectacles.

p.90. Sultan Ahmet III watching a performance by dancing boys.

p.91. Sultan Ahmet III watching dancing boys attired in girl's clothes and grotesque dancers.

p.92. The display of a rope dancer, jesters, dancing boys and stilt dancers with swords.

p.93. Sultan Ahmet III watching a pyrotechnic display taking place on a raft bearing giant puppets.

p.94. Mounted Janissary band *(mehter)* during the Imperial Festival.

p.95. A reclining young man intoxicated by wine.

p.96. Dancing Girl.

By the Same author Dost Yayınları introduces:

La Peinture Miniature Turque. La Période ottomane
(with thirty-nine miniatures in full colour)

Karagöz. Turkish Shadow Theatre
(with eighty-five full colour and eighty black and white illustrations)

Karagöz. Théâtre d'ombres turc
(with eighty-five full colour and hundred forty-nine black and white
illustrations).

A Pictorial History of Turkish Dancing
(with hundred ninety-four illustrations, 101 in colour).

🗿🗿🗿🗿🗿🗿🗿🗿🗿🗿🗿🗿

## ACKNOWLEDGEMENT

The Publisher wishes to thank the following photographers for aid
in securing of transparancies of illustrations: Mustafa Türkyılmaz,
Hamza İnanç, Haluk Doğanbey, Sami Güner and Erkin Emiroğlu.
He is also indebted to Mr. Hilmi Yavuz for kindly reading the
galley proofs and making valuable observations.